5.50

WITHDRAWN

PROBATION WORK
Critical Theory and Socialist Practice

PROBATION WORK
Critical Theory and Socialist Practice

HILARY WALKER
BILL BEAUMONT

Basil Blackwell · Oxford

First published 1981
Basil Blackwell Publisher Limited
108 Cowley Road, Oxford OX4 1JF, England

British Library Cataloguing in Publication Data

Walker, Hilary
   Probation work.
   1. Probation – Great Britain
   I. Title   II. Beaumont, Bill
   364.6'3'0941   HV9346

   ISBN 0–631–12729–1

Phototypesetting by Oxford Publishing Services
Printed in Great Britain by Billing and Sons Limited
Guildford, London, Oxford, Worcester

Contents

Acknowledgements

This book draws on our experience in the probation service over the years and we would like to thank those clients and colleagues who have contributed to our understanding of the work. We have learnt much from our active involvement in union affairs, so thanks go to our friends in struggle within NAPO and NMAG. To some people we are particularly grateful for their encouragement and support during the preparation of this book. We have benefited from the assistance of those friends who read and commented on our draft: John Clarke, Kevin Kirwin, Robin Parker and Helen Schofield. Our thanks also to Joy Kaye and Anne Garry who helped in the arduous job of typing and preparing the manuscript. The people mentioned deserve credit for their contribution to this book but cannot be criticized for its content, responsibility for which, of course, remains with the authors.

PART I PROBATION WORK

1
Something's Wrong

Working as a probation officer is a funny way to make a living. The job involves struggling to solve problems with no apparent solution and trying to reconcile conflicting interests. Your day is spent worrying how to balance demands on your time and choosing between equally un-palatable alternatives. At the end of the day you never feel that a job has been done, let alone well done. Sometimes you wish the work had clear limits, sometimes the restrictions of the role are very frustrating. Time after time the same kind of problem recurs; depression and disillusion-ment readily set in. You long for clarity of purpose, textbook prescriptions that really work, skills that are effective, clients who are eager and responsive. Probation officers rarely coherently voice these issues. Doubts that crop up are set aside because they interfere with the daily routine. Humour, cynicism, intellectualism or even fever-ish activity provide escapes. In these ways probation officers avoid taking stock of their dilemma. We believe it is important to consider these everyday difficulties. So we begin by outlining the most common problems and illu-strate them with some 'scenes from practice'. Unlike case studies or case examples, these don't have tidy, happy endings, but are glimpses of everyday work drawn from our joint experience. We believe they will ring true for practitioners.

When confronted with the range and seriousness of the social and economic problems affecting their clients, pro-bation officers often feel powerless and ineffectual. Nothing in the armoury of skills and resources at their disposal seems capable of bringing about substantial improvements in their clients' lives. They feel that their impact is both minor and marginal. Faced with problems created by powerful institutions, they sometimes find it necessary to go about things in rather devious and roundabout ways to achieve gains for their clients:

Bob was worried about the Smiths. John Smith was serving the remainder of his sentence in a prison 50 miles from home. He had been transferred following disciplinary measures at another prison so a further move was out of the question. The journey to the prison was complicated, involving a change of trains and two bus rides. Betty could manage it every four weeks when the DHSS covered the cost. Once there, Betty often had to wait an hour to get to see John. The length of the visit depended on how crowded the visiting-room was and on the goodwill of the prison officers. Often it lasted only 30 minutes. John and Betty were clearly under strain because they couldn't sort out important family matters during the visits, let alone keep in touch with each others' lives. Bob thought he must do something. He rang the prison probation officer and asked why visiting arrangements were so appalling. She replied that the welfare department couldn't interfere for fear of upsetting the prison officers; the visits room was not their province. The only way Bob could help at all was to back up an application for a welfare visit. Bob discussed this with Betty and reluctantly they decided this was the only way out. They chose to base the application on one of the many problems the couple were facing – whether Betty should have a sterilization operation. Bob arranged the visit on that basis. He took Betty to the prison, although barely able to spare the time. The visit took place in the visiting-room and lasted three-quarters of an hour. Because it was a special welfare visit, Bob had to sit with Betty and John. He was highly embarrassed and tried to strike a balance between appearing to be the concerned probation officer, for the benefit of the prison staff, and trying to pay as little attention as possible to their conversation. Despite the difficulties, Betty and John enjoyed the visit. However welfare visits are a privilege and it is most unlikely that they will get another.

Even when it proves possible to help a particular client, probation officers often recognize that help is limited. They appreciate that the client is only one of many experiencing the same problems. Unable to tackle the wider issues, probation officers feel compelled to do what they can for the individual but are aware of the limitations and dangers of this 'special pleading':

Ray was on probation and had set up home with his girlfriend Kim, who recently had a baby. After much persuasion the council agreed to treat them as a couple and housed them. All the houses in the street were of the same type; compulsorily purchased by the council as part of a new road scheme, sub-standard, in urgent need of repair. Destined for demolition, they were unlikely to be renovated to a reasonable standard. Some said the road would never be built and the starting date was indeed repeatedly postponed as spending cuts hit harder.

Ray and Kim were the only family on the street known to the probation service, and Ray was anxious his neighbours should not know about his criminal record. The probation officer was concerned about the state of the house, especially because it could be affecting the baby's health. So she worked hard with Ray and Kim to try to get them rehoused. The couple wrote to the housing department, their MP, their councillor and got a letter of support from their GP. The probation officer pleaded regularly with the housing department that Ray and Kim were a special case. Ray deserved the support of the community in his rehabilitation. Kim was depressed by the housing conditions, was not coping well and the baby's health might be at risk. Eventually the council agreed to house them in a new maisonette. Ray and Kim were overjoyed. Their probation officer was pleased for them. But her pleasure was tinged with worry about the new home, already showing signs of structural faults and very expensive to heat. Whenever she drove past their old house she felt uneasy about the plight of the families left in the street, and the problems faced by the couple who moved in after Ray and Kim.

Often probation officers are faced with problems that seem to be intractable. Rather than finding useful solutions or constructive ways forward they find themselves 'pouring oil on troubled waters' or 'cooling out the situation'. They encourage the client to talk about the problem or take some action that will divert attention from the immediate crisis, but find this a poor substitute for tackling its cause. At times probation officers, working hard to alleviate distress, wonder if their efforts amount to much more than 'patching-up', which only obscures the true, harsh nature of the system. They wonder if their services would be needed if state benefits were higher or unemployment lower. Feeling 'used' leads probation officers to doubt the value and purpose of their work:

Pete appeared in the Crown Court and was sentenced to three years' imprisonment for jointly stealing a lorry-load of jeans. Perhaps unrealistically he had not anticipated being sent to prison and so family affairs were in a real mess the day he was taken down to the cells. He left behind a wife, Rose, and five children aged between ten years and twelve months. Andy, the probation officer, called a few days later. He found a mountain of work to be done. Finances needed to be juggled as cleverly as possible, and Rose needed advice over visiting. The children were upset and confused about their father's absence and Rose was distraught.

Andy tried to help during the prison sentence but became aware that his efforts were small compared to the family's needs. Supplementary Benefit levels were pitifully inadequate. Andy helped out with a hamper and toys from a local charity at Christmas, and second-hand clothes at other times. He hated giving 'charity', especially when he saw how embarrassed Rose was at needing to accept it. The children missed their father and began playing up; Rose missed her husband but managed to cope with the kids' distress. She became ill through worry and not eating enough, and was slow to recover. The washing machine broke down and the kids were wetting the beds.

Andy gave what he called 'support'. He argued with obstinate gas board officials and awkward DHSS officers on Rose's behalf. One time her giro didn't arrive. The DHSS said it was in the post and refused payment although she was broke. Rose was at the end of her tether and tearfully told Andy she was going down to smash their windows. He calmed her down and arranged a small loan to tide her over until the giro arrived.

Pete began to wonder if Rose was having an affair – not because he had any evidence, it was just that so many other men had received 'dear John' letters. Visits became strained as Pete aggressively questioned Rose about her movements. Anxiety about parole increased the tension. Andy tried to calm Pete and Rose's worries and submitted a parole report emphasizing the positive aspects of circumstances at home. Secretly he doubted whether Pete would get parole. Andy wanted to show the judge who had passed sentence what had happened. He felt he was being used like a dishcloth to mop up the mess someone else had made.

Many probation officers experience a divergence between their personal opinions and values, and those they are expected to uphold. They find that in their work they are expected to advocate the importance of thrift, the work ethic and the benefits of constructive leisure activities – though their own life styles may reflect different values. As public employees and 'servants of the court', probation officers are expected to uphold the law, the authority of the court and the value of probation supervision. But they often have doubts. Sometimes they question the validity of laws, the system of justice and the usefulness of their work:

This is Cathy's fifth court appearance for soliciting and for the first time she has been remanded for a social enquiry report. Already subject to a suspended sentence, she will go to prison unless the probation officer can persuade the court otherwise. Cathy is single and has no children. She left school at the earliest opportunity and her chances of earning much from a regular job are slim. She adopts an instrumental and businesslike approach to prostitution and has progressed from soliciting on the streets to sitting by a window lit by a red lamp. This time she is bitter about her arrest, since she had signalled to a cruising car containing two vice squad officers. She believes she was 'set up'. Her probation officer Lynn is in a dilemma: she thinks that soliciting should be decriminalized; she certainly thinks that imprisoning prostitutes is wrong, but is faced with having to write a report for Cathy's court appearance. The two alternative recommendations she thinks might swing the court away from imprisonment are probation and community service but neither seems appropriate.

Cathy is reluctant to be put on probation, she does not think it can help or change her, and Lynn is inclined to agree. Community service with its philosophy of repaying society for a wrong done seems even more unsuitable; both believe that Cathy already provides a useful service to society.

Probation officers are frustrated to find that the conditions and requirements included in the orders and licences they supervise can make the job even more difficult. Although sometimes ensuring superficial compliance, they often hamper the development of a useful working relationship with clients. All too often, caseloads consist of unwilling conscripts who intend to have as little as possible to do with probation officers. This is not what they had been led to expect – recruitment material, training courses and text-books mentioned 'authority problems' but they were said to be readily overcome. The experience of the job results in a crisis of confidence about the usefulness of social work methods and the structures within which probation officers work:

Larry had gone to Borstal straight from local authority care, having committed burglaries while on the run from a community home. His Borstal licence was transferred to the probation service. At the allocation meeting nobody wanted to take the case. The team was fed up with social services recommending Borstal for difficult kids and wondered if social workers knew what Borstal was like. Phil agreed to take the case; he discovered that Larry had previously been on probation supervision and his probation officer recommended the care order.

Phil tried hard with Larry, though he seemed to be as reluctant to have anything to do with probation officers as they had been to take him on. He phoned the social worker who dealt with him and discovered that she had been unable to find a local authority placement for Larry, and recommended Borstal as a last resort. Phil visited Larry regularly in Borstal but he remained sullen and uncommunicative. He visited Larry's mother who agreed to have him back home. Phil thought this was marginally better than either of the hostels available. Larry said he wanted to live in his own flat but agreed to go home. On home leave Larry didn't come in to see Phil, who feared the worst for his discharge. As expected, Larry rarely called into the office and usually managed to come when Phil was out visiting. Larry obviously resented the conditions of his Borstal licence; he reckoned he had served his sentence and should be left alone to get on with his life. Larry's mother regularly phoned the office full of complaints about her son's behaviour at home, late hours and untidiness. He wouldn't work; he wouldn't eat the good food she put in front of him; he was a bad influence on her younger kids. Phil tried to calm her; although the arrangement wasn't working out, Phil didn't know where else to put him. Larry brushed aside his mother's complaints when Phil tried to discuss them and called his mother a nagging, fussy old woman. (Secretly Phil agreed but thought he had better not tell Larry.) Eventually Larry stopped coming into the office at all; Phil called at the house on the advice of his senior, who thought these things should be chased up. Larry had left home and Phil had to face a barrage of abuse about the uselessness of probation officers before he made his escape. Phil's senior was none too happy about the situation and wanted to report Larry's disappearance. Phil thought that Larry should be given more time: he hadn't (yet) re-offended and it might be better for him to find his feet on his own. Certainly putting him back in Borstal wouldn't help. The senior said that Larry was clearly flouting the conditions of his licence and should be reminded he couldn't get away with this. A report recommending recall was submitted to the Home Office.

CRISIS OF CONFIDENCE

We have outlined some of the major dilemmas probation officers experience in their work. These are rarely exposed to open and rational debate but rather find expression in general restlessness, dissatisfaction and disaffection among probation officers. This 'crisis of confidence' has been recognized and there have been various attempts, from very different points of view, to provide explanations for its development. Each of these generates a solution – a means of curing the probation service of its ills. Here we outline some of the more familiar strands in the 'crisis of confidence' debate.

One theme that recurs is that of student probation officer selection and training. It is claimed that too many students are 'in their earlys 20s . . . motivated by very Left-wing political values and looking forward to a socialist utopia when the poor will literally no longer be with us'.[1] This could apparently be remedied by the recruitment of 'older social work students', of whom 'very few thought or spoke in those terms'.[2] Training courses are said to equip probation officers inadequately for the nitty-gritty of the job. Peter Bibby writes:

> It is not too much of a caricature to say that social workers and heads of field work departments want people to come off social work courses as qualified technicians ready to do the job with their feet on the ground, and that training courses produce theoreticians with their heads in the clouds. Unfortunately, very often the clouds are always more than six feet above the ground, so the head and feet are never joined.[3]

He expects the product of a training course to be: 'able to write English, serve Probation Orders, know something about Breach of Probation and how to take the oath in court, and perhaps even wear a suit!!!'[4]

The solution is obvious – courses should be changed so they produce probation officers who will carry out the routine tasks of the job unquestioningly.

The theme of immaturity and youth as a cause of these problems continues after the completion of training. One chief probation officer asserts:

> Youth is a wonderful thing; new blood and new brooms are most desirable attributes. But the infusion of too much blood can give rise to difficulties. The institution which suffers it may lose hold on those 'self-evident' assumptions which were once the core of its being. Its sense of purpose may become diffused and confused.[5]

He explains why young probation officers are confused:

> Pretty well all my generation in the probation service are second careerists. We had sorted out most of our basic emotional and intellectual problems, so far as we were

likely to, before we joined. People coming straight from university or polytechnic have to do it on the job: no easy task.[6]

David Mathieson echoes this theme: 'Far from embracing the hallowed traditions and structures of the past, many young officers are eager to impose their own influence on the Service, often with quite disruptive effects.'[7] He also questions their personal stability. The kinds of solutions these commentators advocate are the recruitment of older, more mature staff who will contribute personal stability and knuckle down to the demands of the organization; and the provision of counsellors to 'social work' those who need help in adjusting to reality.

Others suggest that this 'crisis of confidence' occurs because probation officers lack faith in themselves and their skills. Loz Coates writes:

> the probation officer . . . seems uncertain and insecure in this role by reason of the changes that have taken place in recent years. What is needed now is to define a special unique treatment role for the open treatment of delinquency in the community and a confidence in the professionalism of probation and its conceptual framework.[8]

David Millard develops the theme of confidence and sees achieving this as a personal battle. He quotes Bill Jordan approvingly:

> We have to be willing to experience tensions and contradictions, to behave oddly or badly, and willing for the client to recognise this; and then we have to find the strength to recover, with them, and in finding our own way back, to help them to find theirs.[9]

These commentators see the solution in a new confidence, based on belief in professional skills.

Some claim that if only the right social work method or approach were adopted, professional confidence would

return. 'Social work entrepreneurs' assert that their
particular method will deal with all the difficulties
experienced in the past.[10] A variant of this theme is the
search for a 'radical social work'. As new approaches arrive
on the scene they tend to be grasped hopefully, but similar
problems arise. Despite past disappointments the search
for the 'new improved' method continues.

Another approach is to blame depression on high caseloads, too much work and insufficient resources – if only we
had more staff, enough money and plenty of time, we could
do the job properly. While it is true that insufficient funds
and overwork have presented real and serious problems for
the probation service, there is little to suggest that resolution of this difficulty would solve the kinds of dilemmas we
have described.

Some commentators believe that the system of management in the probation service is a main cause of discontent
and disillusionment. The NAPO Members Action Group
(NMAG), a left-wing pressure group within the probation
officers' union – the National Association of Probation
Officers (NAPO) – voices some familiar complaints:

> The Probation Service has changed out of all recognition
> since its simple beginnings . . . we have seen the intro-
> duction of intermediate grades of management . . . this
> kind of bureaucracy creates a number of problems . . . it
> isolates the worker from the overall controller, which
> leads to frustration and a feeling of impotence because
> the worker has little influence over the policy of the
> organisation and any complaints seem to get lost in the
> chain of communication.[11]

The solution to this is said to be less management, more
democracy and greater importance attached to the role of
the main grade probation officer. The arguments are per-
suasive:

> In the ideal probation service, the practitioners would
> have control over their own affairs. Teams would organise

the distribution of their work and elected representatives would decide their area policy. There would still be a need for planners and people to set up projects but this would reflect the expressed need of the practitioners, and representatives would be answerable to their teams.[12]

Not surprisingly there are also those who see stronger, more effective management as the solution to dissatisfaction:

we believe the service requires positive leadership and that those upon whom this responsibility falls need to be helped to acquire the appropriate skills to develop the full potential of their staffs in order that the needs of all concerned, the courts, the community, the resource providers and the clients themselves are met satisfactorily.[13]

We are not satisfied that the familiar explanations and solutions we have outlined either individually or taken together adequately deal with the 'crisis of confidence' experienced in the probation service. Some appear to us to have merit, others we reject entirely. They all share the limitation of addressing only internal matters and failing to confront more fundamental issues about probation work and its place in society. Ultimately they do not help probation officers to understand and deal with the problems experienced in everyday practice. We believe that a more radical and fundamental approach is needed to these problems and this is what we hope to offer in this book.

First we examine the everyday work of probation officers in detail, contrasting the official account with the real practice experience and highlighting important issues. Then we attempt to explain these by reaching for an understanding of the role of the probation service in a social, economic and political context. We conclude by discussing the implications of this for the practising probation officer, and offer some suggestions for approaching the work.

We have arrived at this stage in our thinking through the experience of working as probation officers, having begun in the probation service with very different ideas. But through our doubts, confusion, anger and uncertainty we have tried to make some sense of the job. Our search for an adequate understanding has been a gradual process over a number of years and we have been helped by discussion with others and by background reading. When we have used material from other sources in illustration we have done so because it connected with our experience and seemed useful.

Our concern is to examine probation work in a wider context than conventional social work theory permits. We do not therefore attempt a detailed critical analysis of social work theory but will pay some attention to 'methods', which often pass for theory in social work. We have made little use of foreign literature. Although there are similarities between the criminal justice system in this country and others, particularly America, there are significant differences and we think our arguments are better made by the use of material from Great Britain. We have not been able to deal with some important issues. In particular, for reasons of space we have not been able to analyse the historical development of the probation service, although we see a clear need for a more critical approach than that provided in the conventional histories. Probation in Scotland and Northern Ireland have been left out because they require particular attention. Domestic and juvenile work have also been omitted, mainly because of space limitations, but we also consider that domestic work is sufficiently different from other work to need separate treatment. Juvenile work, like domestic work, involves consideration of issues about children, the family, good parenting and youth which, although connected to many aspects of our analysis, do need special attention. We have now set the scene for the rest of the book by explaining our starting point – the problems experienced in the job, and by outlining our general approach.

In the next two chapters we examine in some detail the major tasks which make up probation officers' working lives and identify more clearly the problems encountered. First we consider the official accounts of these tasks, drawing on Home Office circulars, government reports and accepted authorities on the probation service, including professional and academic accounts. From all these sources we build a picture of the job as it is supposed to be – the official account. Then from our own experience, and the few existing articulated 'grass-roots' accounts, we present our view of the job as it is really experienced – the practice account. The official and practice accounts contrast sharply. We seek to highlight the disparities between the two and discuss some of the reasons for this divergence. Our detailed consideration of these major tasks begins to locate and identify the contradictions we believe to be inherent in the role of the probation officer. We return to examine the source of these contradictions in our theoretical work in the second part of the book.

2
Court-Based Work

In this chapter we examine the preparation of social enquiry reports and the supervision of probation orders. In the next we examine after-care and prison welfare, both prison-based tasks. The tasks examined in this chapter historically form the foundation of probation work, emerging in changed form from the activities of the police court missionaries. Both originate from the courts and are often identified as the more progressive, helpful and constructive work of the probation service. Space precludes us from dealing exhaustively with all aspects and our intention is to highlight those aspects which lead to an understanding of the strains and conflicts experienced by probation officers.

SOCIAL ENQUIRY REPORTS

The Official Account

Preparing social enquiry reports accounts for about 10 per cent of probation service work;[1] in 1976, 215,000 were completed.[2] The official definition is well established – the Streatfeild Report said:

> the first function of a probation report is to provide information about the offender and his background which will help the court in determining the most suitable method of dealing with him.[3]

It also specified the purpose of that information; it should be relevant both to the court's assessment of culpability and to consideration of how the offender's criminal career might be checked. The report should contain an opinion as to the likely effect on the subject's criminal career of probation or other forms of treatment and be based on comprehensive and reliable information about offenders. Drawing on these Streatfeild criteria, reinforced by Home Office circulars, Mathieson and Walker assert: 'the true nature of a social enquiry report is a comprehensive and objective document prepared by the professionally trained social worker of the court'.[4] These important characteristics of the modern report are often highlighted in the literature by comparison with probation officers' earlier efforts, described by Carlen and Powell as verbal pleas made 'explicitly and without embarrassment on behalf of certain defendants',[5] and based, according to Jarvis, on 'hope or intuition or emotional involvement'.[6]

Professional accounts suggest that reports are more than just sentencing aids: they are a diagnostic process enabling offenders to be matched with appropriate treatment. Joan King counsels probation officers against over-identification with the client because 'such departures from impartiality are unlikely to lead to the form of treatment most helpful to the offender in the long run.'[7]

This view of the social enquiry report has led a few probation areas to establish intake teams to 'provide an improved diagnostic service to the courts'.[8] Treatment is regarded as synonymous with sentence because the professional literature assumes there is no conflict between the interests of individual offenders and those of society. Mathieson and Walker acknowledge the difficulty of maintaining objectivity but explain that 'the needs of society and of the client which on the surface appear conflicting, when analysed are complementary; society requires its criminals to be reformed and the client requires his problems to be solved'.[9] By preparing a report in a professional manner 'the probation officer is the one who enables both sets of requirements to be fulfilled'.[10]

We have now identified all the elements in the official account of the social enquiry report. Reports should be (1) reliable, (2) comprehensive and (3) objective. In order to assist the court in deciding upon the most appropriate sentence they should (4) be relevant to the court's sentencing function, (5) match offenders with the correct form of treatment and thus (6) enable the needs of both society and the offender to be met.

The Practice Account

Before examining the elements of the official account in the light of practice it is appropriate to make a few general points. It is not unusual for a probation officer to complete 80–100 reports per year or to have up to eight reports on the go at the same time. Davies and Knopf showed that an average report was completed in about four and a half hours with only one-third of that time spent in interviewing the subject.[11] Interviews often take place in less than relaxed surroundings – the probation officer having to fight off interruptions from children, the television, neighbours and animals. It is not easy to concentrate with a demented budgie sitting on your head or a large Alsatian sniffing up your skirt. The probation officer has to reach a judgement quickly, often starting completely from scratch. The offender is usually preoccupied with unresolved issues about arrest, conviction, or problems unrelated to the court appearance. In practice social enquiry reports are often hasty judgements made under considerable pressure, on the basis of inadequate information. Since the probation officer completes many reports, choosing recommendations from a small range of possibilities, it is not surprising that reports emerge in a highly routinized (though sometimes idiosyncratic) conceptual form.

Reliability

In his study of social enquiry reports, Fred Perry found that: 'the provision of the most basic material . . . was haphazard and unreliable'.[12] This confirms the impression from practice that most reports are based primarily on information provided by the offender and not corroborated from any source beyond a quick glance at police antecedents or old probation records. There are some obvious practical reasons why probation officers do not check information. Sometimes a broad picture, for instance of the offender's employment history, seems more relevant than an exhaustively checked list. Some material is difficult to corroborate (e.g. educational achievement of older people) or is essentially subjective (e.g. family experience). Sometimes checks are inappropriate: it would be counter-productive to contact a current employer who might then sack an offender. Having made such qualifications it remains significant that most probation officers make little effort to check important information given to them by offenders.

This is not because in their experience information gathered has proved so reliable that probation officers decide that checking is unnecessary. Most have had the experience of checking 'facts' which turn out to be false. On the whole they learn not to risk disruption of the picture they have built up from their interview. In practice, probation officers place relatively little importance on the reliability of reports and are more concerned with their overall effect. They concentrate on presenting material which will be convincing and will not be contradicted in court – to be caught in error would not only be embarrassing and reduce credibility in general but would also undermine the effect of that particular report.

Comprehensiveness

Perry similarly points to the lack of comprehensiveness he found in reports. In 200 Crown Court reports studied 'apart from the name of client, address and date of birth there were no facts which were universally present in the sample'.[13] A recent Home Office Research Study of social enquiry reports, using a wider sample than Perry, produced a similar finding.[14] Although such studies can be criticized for a failure to distinguish universally applicable categories of information, it is true that in practice little emphasis is placed on comprehensiveness. Reports are usually quite short, rarely more than two pages, in contrast to the exhaustive 'pre-sentence' reports compiled by American probation officers. In fact courts have little patience with longer reports – a magistrate commenting on Perry's research says: 'the court does not wish to be over-whelmed with facts. The probation officer must surely learn to exercise a sense of relevance.'[15] The official goal of comprehensiveness is therefore limited by common con-sent between the courts and the probation service.

The selection of information by probation officers for inclusion in reports is by no means random. Information is included or discarded in order to shape the particular pic-ture of the client which the probation officer hopes to convey. Favourable information – for example about the defendant's involvement in voluntary work or role per-formance as a parent – may be included or highlighted to evoke a sympathetic reaction from the bench. Knowledge about a client's claiming social security whilst in employ-ment may be excluded, to avoid a punitive response. Pearce and Wareham state that such purposiveness in the omission and selection of information is aimed at justifying the particular recommendation made in the report.[16] Probation officers, far from pursuing the official goal of comprehensiveness, make use of the need to be selective in order to shape their reports in an attempt to make them more effective.

Objectivity

The goal of objectivity is problematic because the probation officer is inevitably affected by human contact with the client and cannot remain detached. As Perry puts it: 'How-ever high the integrity of the participants might be, objec-tivity is an impossible expectation in human exchanges, and as long as it continues to be the unquestioned criterion in presentence reporting, there will be an ambiguity inherent in the process'.[17]

The judgements the probation officer has to make are not abstract ones: they have real and immediate practical con-sequences. Most probation officers have strong feelings about the criminal justice system and the effects of sentences. While they acknowledge and pay lip-service to the official expectation of objectivity, probation officers find it impossible in practice and instead shape their reports to their own purposes. Recognizing this ambiguity, Pearce and Wareham describe the objectivity of the social enquiry report as a 'tenuous mythology'.[18]

Relevance to the Courts' Sentencing Function

According to Perry, information relevant to sentencing is often missing from reports. Many probation officers in his study rated their knowledge of the client's offence (information relevant to assessment of culpability) as 'less than good'. In 87 per cent of reports there was no mention of the client's capacity for change; in 80 per cent no assessment of the risk of further delinquency, and comment on the prospects of checking the offender's criminal career was seldom included.[19] Perry suggests that: 'the relevance of the information communicated to the court by social workers is largely left to the professional discretion of the social worker and is therefore substantially affected by their professional ideology'.[20]

We have already suggested that far from being comprehensive documents, social enquiry reports have a purposively selected content. Information relevant to culpability and further delinquency is likely to be particularly speculative, sensitive and prejudical. The omission of such material may be similarly purposive, avoiding a difficult assessment which would disrupt the picture the probation officer is seeking to present.

Offender–Treatment Matching

The official goal of the social enquiry report, uniquely to match each client with the necessary and appropriate form of treatment, confuses the idea of treatment with that of sentence. It ignores the fact that the court will impose a sentence chosen from a narrow range of options, most of which cannot by any stretch of the imagination be considered a form of treatment. Probation officers are mostly

acutely aware of these limitations and of their involvement
in a criminal justice system which has goals other than to
meet the needs of their clients. In the sentencing process
these are clearly secondary to the courts' other pre-occupa-
tions – retribution, deterrence and legal justice. The constraints surrounding the preparation of reports make them
unlikely instruments for diagnosis.

The idea of the social enquiry report as a 'moment for
diagnosis' draws heavily on the analogy with medical
treatment. The application of this model to criminal behaviour has been subject to sustained criticism recently
even from within the Home Office Research Unit.[21] Some
probation officers have always preferred a more 'common
sense' view of their work, to the treatment model taught on
many training courses. Most have been forced by their
experience of practice to doubt the relevance of a diagnosis/
treatment model of intervention. Consequently probation
officers adopt a pragmatic approach to social enquiry
reports, rather than the diagnostic model advanced in
official accounts.

Congruent Needs of Offenders and Society

The suggestion that the interests of offenders and society
are really complementary is based on a view of delinquency
as an illness which both would be better without. The
criminal act is seen as a piece of personal maladjustment
rather than a conscious act with social and economic significance. This model of delinquency requires the adoption of
an extreme consensus view of society – all have a stake and
can benefit so only the maladjusted dissent from its
common values and goals.

The practical experience of probation officers sharply
contradicts that view. The whole ritual of the court makes it
clear that the offender is in conflict with 'society'. Decisions
are made which are directly against the interests of the
individual offender 'for the greater good of all'. Offenders'
definitions are irrelevant and only the courts' are legitimate.
Sentences are imposed which, far from solving offenders'

problems, merely add to them. In these circumstances the social enquiry report cannot be an instrument of reconciliation and probation officers are generally clear that this is not a realistic aim.

Social Enquiry Reports – A Discussion

We have shown that the official account does not accord with the practice of probation officers and indeed is widely disregarded by them. We need to understand this discrepancy between official expectations and actual practice. Many studies of reports have treated them as if they were a straightforward analysis by the probation officer of the reasons for an individual's criminal act and the most effective course of treatment to prevent a repetition. We suggest that in fact the dominant influence on reports is that they are written for an *audience* – the court. This determines the approach taken, the content and the style. It also acts as a constraint, determining the limit of material considered relevant.

Pearce and Wareham criticize other research for assuming that the purpose of a social enquiry report is clear: 'Social Enquiry Report content is only comprehensible in the context of the probation officer's purpose in preparing the report'.[22]

We have made it clear that probation officers are concerned about the effect of their reports on their audience. Their purpose in writing reports is twofold: to influence the sentence imposed and at the same time to maintain credibility with the court.

We have shown that the official account rests on the assumption of a consensus in society which is contradicted by practice. Probation officers accumulate information in the job (from clients, colleagues, written material and observation) which makes them uneasy about the system of criminal justice. Doubts about the need for particular laws, discrimination in the application of the law, police methods, the way in which guilt is established and differences in punishment imposed on different types of offenders – all contribute to this uneasiness. For all these reasons probation officers tend to see their reports as a *means of redressing the balance by influencing the courts towards more lenient sentences.*

Not surprisingly probation officers find some conflict between their attempt to influence towards leniency and their need to maintain credibility. Pearce and Wareham suggest that probation officers have two operational definitions of their role in preparing reports: the front region account which corresponds with the official account and is offered to magistrates, researchers, etc. and the back region account 'where the impression fostered by the public performance is contradicted and the suppressed facts make an appearance'.[23]

The back region account is used among colleagues and the informal rules which influence report writing are acknowledged. We suggest that probation officers frequently knowingly use the official account to mask their real motivation and practice. Thus, when Pauline Hardiker identifies three roles adopted by probation officers in writing reports (classical justice, advising the court and social work), she does no more than identify three tactics used by probation officers to influence the court. Significantly she comments that:

> part of the explanation for probation officers adopting a more active social work role in their social enquiry reports was that the offender's criminal record and personal circumstances were so serious that custody was likely and an attempt was being made to keep him out of prison.[24]

The attempt to prevent a prison sentence is validated and made respectable by the use of the social work role. The existence of these front and back region accounts explains some of the problems encountered by researchers in this area.

The need to maintain credibility with their audience determines much of the content of reports and the extent to which probation officers are able to pursue the goal of achieving lenient sentences. Carlen and Powell identify some of the strategies adopted for maintaining credibility. These include filtering (purposive selection of material), tickling (respectful recognition of the courts' viewpoint by the use of phrases such as 'whilst not underestimating the seriousness of the offence' in order to open the way for more radical recommendations) and reference to authoritative knowledge.[25] As well as these devices which make reports curious documents to read, probation officers attempt to 'second guess' the courts' probable sentences in making recommendations. The overall content of the report stays close to the courts' own probable definition of relevance. Occasionally a probation officer may even feel the need to recommend imprisonment in a difficult case, in order to retain general credibility.

In the courts the focus is on the individual defendant, the individual criminal act, the defendant's guilt, criminal responsibility, criminal record and background history. Criminal acts are viewed purely as a particular aspect of an individual's behaviour and not as a more widespread social phenomenon with social, economic and political causes. Probation officers operate within that *individualized system of criminal justice* and maintain that perspective. They must remain within the limits of relevance set by the courts – social and structural problems can be included only as a description of individual circumstances. For instance, the poor housing situation of an individual offender can be described and may evoke sympathy but comment about the way in which market forces systematically disadvantage certain groups would be unacceptable. Carlen and Powell quote a magistrate who makes this explicit:

> One probation officer made a reference to capitalism and marxism . . . you know, capitalist society, that sort of thing . . . you know. And I had to say – that won't do – I don't care about the politics of a probation officer but the defendant has to see the report and that kind of thing isn't appropriate to a relationship of . . . uh . . . treatment.[26]

Probation officers may hold a more general perspective and see a particular client as representative of a group or class of people (black, unemployed, poor, youth, etc.). They may be critical of the justice system or even perceive class differentiation in that system. But they are constrained by the process of individualization. They must act within the limits set by the court or be quickly discredited. They may perceive many problems within the social system but have to resort to *special pleading* on behalf of their clients, which reinforces the individualized nature of the justice system.

PROBATION ORDERS

The Official Account

The supervision of probation orders is the most long-standing of probation officers' tasks and remains their major activity, accounting for about 18 per cent of a main grade officer's time, the largest portion of time allocated to any one area of work.[27] The Morison Report provides an official definition of probation:

> We understand by probation the submission of an offender while at liberty to a specified period of supervision by a social caseworker who is an officer of the court; during this period the offender remains liable if not of good conduct to be otherwise dealt with by the court.[28]

The report says probation epitomizes the principle of minimum interference with the life and liberty of the offender, whilst at the same time showing disapproval of, and protecting society from, the wrongdoer. It both represents society's standards and offers help to those who fail to attain them. Probation:

> seeks to protect society through the supervision to which the offender is required to submit, it both minimizes the

restriction placed on him and offers him the help of
society in adjusting his conduct to its demands. . . . The
offender is conditionally entrusted with freedom so that
he may learn the social duties it involves.[29]

The value of probation to the community is particularly
emphasized:

Probation extracts from the offender a contribution
within the limits of his capacity, to the wellbeing of
others, whether it be through his useful employment in
the community or through his participation in the life of
the family or other social group. In so doing it minimises
the economic and social disruption caused by the probationer's offence . . . and seeks to avoid the harm to
others that follows for example the imprisonment of a
breadwinner.[30]

Being allowed to remain in the community is conditional
on the offender's supervision by a probation officer and
meeting the requirements of a probation order. The duties
of the probation officer in respect of supervision are laid
down in the Probation Rules 1965.[31] The primary and most
familiar duty is to 'advise, assist and befriend' but more
detailed expectations are also outlined. Regarding contact,
the probation officer is expected to keep in close touch with
probationers, meet them frequently and require them to
report at stated intervals. The frequency of meetings is to be
determined amongst other circumstances by the behaviour
and progress of the probationer, with contact particularly
intensive at the beginning of the order. For the offender's
general welfare the probation officer is expected to:
'encourage a person on probation to make use of any statutory or voluntary agency which might contribute to his
welfare, and to take advantage of any available social,
recreational or educational facilities suited to his age, ability
and temperament'.[32] The probation officer is expected,
when appropriate, to ensure that the probationer is in suitable and regular employment. Although these duties are set

out very formally in the Probation Rules, they are really
guidelines to be operated with discretion. The Morison
Report states: 'The probation officer must in our view be
conceded reasonable discretion to use the supervisory
technique he thinks best'.[33]

In official literature the probation officer is clearly identified as an officer of the court entrusted with the supervision
of probationers and accountable to the court. A recent
CCETSW document says:

> The probation officer has a duty to advise, assist and
> befriend the client and to supervise his response to the
> Order on behalf of the Court. This duty is undertaken on
> the basis of social work principles but the nature of the
> Order implies recognition of the Courts' authority.
> Should the client fail to meet the requirements of the
> Order the officer is obliged to consider imposing sanc-
> tions which may require the client to be returned to the
> Court to be sentenced again.[34]

Although official accounts concede probation officers' flexibility and discretion in the methods they use there is an
expectation that they will always act as agents of the court.

The requirements the probation officer is expected to
enforce state that the probationer should be of good behaviour and lead an industrious life; should inform the
probation officer of any change of residence or employment; keep in touch with the probation officer as directed;
and receive visits at home as requested. Additional
requirements such as receiving psychiatric treatment,
residence at a hostel or where the probation officer directs,
or attendance at a day training centre can be included.
Courts also have the power to insert any other requirements
they consider suitable – for example imposing restrictions
on a probationer's associates, haunts or habits. A probation
order can only be made if the offender consents. Official
accounts see these requirements as a framework for intervention, enabling help, advice and control to be delivered.
The restrictions imposed are seen as a necessary condition

for liberty and of benefit to the offender who, through contact with the probation officer and by keeping the conditions of the order, will learn a more conforming and therefore a more satisfactory way of life.

The purpose of probation, and the expectation placed on the probation officer, is that supervision will effect some permanent change in the offender. Jarvis quotes Swanson who says that the aim of probation is: 'a more permanent goal than inhibition under authoritative restraint of criminal or otherwise antisocial conduct during the limited period of recognisance, that is the permanent assumption of a stable and responsible manner of living'.[35]

When making an order the court must consider that the offender is in need of such attention. The change expected as a result of supervision is the reformation of the client to meet the demands of society. Mark Monger writes:

> the desire of the court in making the order is that the offender shall be assisted in whatever ways will result in his remaining a law abiding citizen; there is also the implied hope and expectation that he will become a happier and more stable person; but it is the needs of society which are of primary importance.[36]

Clearly, acceptance and conformity to one's place in society is of prime importance.

Official accounts emphasize that there are two closely linked components to probation orders: care and control. The court invests authority in the probation officer to ensure that the order's requirements are fulfilled. This use of authority and control is said to demonstrate the care and concern of society for the probationer. Joan King writes: 'the probation order is both a limitation of the offender's freedom and an expression of concern for his wellbeing' and 'requirements and restrictions are imposed with the intention of helping rather than punishing'.[37]

Just as care and control are seen as complementary so there is assumed to be a real community of interest between the offender and society. The offender may seem to be at

odds with society and authority but the probation officer,
by exerting firm, consistent and benevolent control, will
help the client come to terms with authority problems.
Morison points out that the probation officer is an agent of
society and claims that: 'the offender cannot achieve his
potential for contented living while he is at odds with
society and one of the probation officer's tasks is to help him
perceive that in this sense his interests and those of society
are identical'.[38]

Both official and professional literature place considerable emphasis on the use of social casework within the
framework of probation orders. Little has been written by
professionals about supervision of probation orders. Both
the major texts, *Casework in Probation* by Mark Monger[39] and
Authority in Social Casework by Foren and Bailey,[40] rely
heavily on the use of casework as a method and differ little
in approach from official accounts. They reinforce the
picture of the probation officer as a benevolent authority
figure and lay particular emphasis on the use of charisma
and personal authority in mediating between society and
the client. More recently this exclusive concentration on
casework in the professional literature has given way to
consideration of other social work methods, such as group
work. These fit less closely the individual form of the probation order and have already attracted criticism from the
Central Council of Probation and After-Care Committees.[41]
Nevertheless professional attention has remained focused
on the search for new, more effective social work methods.

We can now summarize the three strands of the official
account of the probation order. Through (1) supervision of
offenders in the community, enforcing requirements and
with sanctions for non-compliance and (2) the practice of
social casework the probation officer is to (3) bring about
permanent change in the offender who is then expected to
meet the demands of society.

The Practice Account

Before examining the three strands of the official account in the light of practice, it is appropriate to make some preliminary general points. In real life, probation has little resemblance to the careful, planned activity of the official accounts. More often probation supervision comprises a series of rushed and superficial routine meetings. Work with probationers competes with other demands on probation officers' time and attention, and urgent tasks such as report writing sometimes take priority. Most clients are seen on a 'reporting evening' at the end of the working day. They can become names on a list to be ticked off if they turn up or added to next week's list (and in line for a reminder letter) if they do not. The problems brought to the probation officer are often practical ones: homeless yet again, the gas or electricity about to be disconnected or the social security causing hassles. The probation officers' limited influence is sought – set an official to influence an official – and at least the office phone works better than the call box. The job frequently dissolves into a hotchpotch of tasks which are never mentioned in the official account or on training courses.

Supervision

A recent Home Office study of time spent on probation clients revealed that supervision is sketchy: the average time spent on each probationer (including travelling) was about 2.1 hours per month or 50 hours per two-year order[42] – hardly the close contact expected. For supervision to be carried out as envisaged, more time would be required as well as new approaches to surveillance. The probation officer's knowledge of the offender's life style and general situation is generally limited to the client's own account and material gleaned from home visits. It is only natural that probationers seek to reassure their supervisors by presenting themselves in the most favourable light. More accurate information would involve unacceptable intrusions on individual privacy. Probation officers have a vested interest in maintaining a favourable picture of the client: to delve too deeply may face the officer with awkward moral choices and this pinpoints the contradiction between the roles of 'officer of the court' and 'befriender of the client'.

A consumer survey by Nottingham probation officers reported that probation was generally described as: 'a five minute talk which was unrelated to the rest of their activities and which because it happened infrequently (although definitions of frequency varied, e.g. only once a month to only once a week) could not therefore have any impact'.[43] The most extreme example of the failure to meet official expectations of supervision is the growing practice of deciding that some probationers will receive nominal supervision or none at all. This is done with the support of, or at the instigation of, management. These cases are described as 'category C', 'low need', or 'on ice'. Various explanations are put forward to account for this decision, the most frequent being the efficient use of resources. Whatever the explanation, it is clear that this way of dealing with probation orders does not accord with the official account.

Many probation officers now argue that they are not 'officers of the court' and prefer to explain their actions and decisions in terms of professional judgement or autonomy. Even those who acknowledge the title do not, on closer examination, behave accordingly. An example is breach proceedings for failure to comply with the conditions of probation. Most probation officers will recognize the truth of Philip Bean's research finding that at some time all probationers breach some condition of their order.[44] Yet recent figures suggests that: 'Action for failure to comply with the conditions of probation orders appears to be taken but rarely – it is understood that the figure is approximately 2%'.[45]

This situation arises not simply because of probation officers' wilful refusal to do their job but because of the difficulties in ensuring that the requirements of probation orders are observed. Special requirements are particularly difficult to enforce. They have been rare but are not unknown and are perhaps becoming more popular with sentencers. Recently magistrates at Chard, Somerset, included in a probation order a condition that the probationer should take a bath once a week.[46] Perhaps the imaginative reader could devise ways for the probation officer to enforce this condition. NAPO's response to the Younger Report describes difficulties familiar to all probation officers:

> It is already possible to include various additional requirements in a probation order but our experience shows that they do not work very well. If you require a young man to take a particular job he can obey you and then get himself the sack. If you forbid him to frequent a particular place he will take a chance that he will not be spotted and usually he will get away with it.[47]

Even the standard conditions requiring good behaviour and promoting industriousness are difficult to enforce in practice. Geoffrey Pearson identified not enforcing the conditions of probation orders as a main category of what he describes as 'official rule breaking'.[48] Probation officers are reluctant to enforce requirements if they believe that to do so could cause difficulties for the client. For instance, the expectation of taking employment may be ignored if the client is able only to get boring, low-paid and unpleasant work.

The best-known duty of probation officers is to advise, assist and befriend – but this familiar role contains hidden difficulties. Befriending implies a voluntary relationship, intimacy, an open-ended commitment, benevolence, warmth. Yet probation officers are paid employees, working a specified and limited number of hours per week. They are expected to carry out the contradictory task of befriending as part of their job. Clients are often confused by their attempts, and may be suspicious or build up unrealistic expectations of what this befriending will involve. They may find it difficult to understand the restrictions and limitations that probation officers must necessarily impose. Probation officers, too, may get involved in confusing and complicated situations if 'befriending' gets out of hand — or if clients step out of the client role as a result.

The Probation Rules, which are supposed to govern the actions of probation officers in carrying out their job, are simply not known and are consequently largely ignored by probation officers and their management. Neither are they as straightforward as they may appear. The duty to help a client take advantage of 'social' recreational or educational facilities suited to his age, ability or temperament' at first sight seems a reasonable task but closer examination reveals considerable difficulties. For many of the people the probation service deals with, education has meant little apart from the imposition of a routine, standards and an alien process that most avoid by one means or another, as Paul Corrigan graphically describes.[49] Those probation clients who wish to return to full-time education, perhaps hoping for an escape route from the round of unskilled labouring jobs, find that opportunities are few. Relevant courses and funding are scarce and vulnerable to cuts when the axe falls on public spending. A similar story can be told about recreational facilities. The probation clientele is often described as 'unclubbable': they tend to choose to spend their leisure time 'hanging around' or in commercial premises rather than in organized youth clubs. The facilities envisaged in the Probation Rules are avoided by many working-class kids because, like education, they are experienced as an imposition of rules, standards and values. Those that do exist are often unattractive and poorly funded. The range suggested in the Probation Rules simply does not exist, making this duty little more than an empty gesture.

Casework with those under Supervision

The first doubt to raise about this aspect of the probation officer's job is the feasibility of casework within the probation setting. Foren and Bailey provide a quotation from Carl Rogers which highlights the difficulties:

> Is it possible for the probation officer to be a counsellor . . . if he is responsible for deciding whether the indi-

vidual has broken probation and hence is to be sent to an institution? . . . It seems to the writer that the counsellor cannot maintain a counselling relationship with the client and at the same time have authority over him. Therapy and authority cannot be co-existent in the same relation-ship. There cannot be an atmosphere of complete per-missiveness when the relationship is authoritative. . . . If the delinquent accepts a counselling relationship with the probation officer and tells him of further delin-quencies the worker must at once decide if he is therapist or officer. . . . The counselling relationship is one in which warmth of acceptance and absence of coercion or personal pressure on the part of the counsellor permits the maximum expression of feelings, attitudes and problems by the counselee. . . .[50]

Rogers can be criticized for creating an idealist picture of therapy, to which few can really aspire, but there is little doubt that the constraints he describes present formidable obstacles to the probation officer. In addition the clients who come through the doors of probation offices are generally not the kind of material that caseworkers are looking for. They are reluctant conscripts to the treatment process, unmotivated towards introspection and unused to expressing their feelings. Geoffrey Parkinson writes: 'My clients cannot accept insight; even if they understood what I was trying to get at, the experience would be too claustro-phobic for them'.[51]

Many clients fail to understand the supposed connection between the offence and the casework the probation officer is trying to involve them in. An articulate consumer in the Nottingham survey said: 'As far as I'm concerned, proba-tion didn't do me any good at all, I really don't see what it does. . . . Perhaps if you're going to open up and tell problems – I don't even tell my mother my problems. It didn't worry me but it didn't do me any good.'[52]

In practice the work done by probation officers seldom justifies the 'casework' label; the situation is nearer than described by Geoffrey Parkinson:

The probation service is crammed full of dedicated
officers who have an accumulation of complex though
partial and half digested psychoanalytic theories and insights into human behaviour. Well meaning, they
blunder their way through their caseloads hoping it all
makes some kind of sense.[53]

Rather than casework probation officers pursue a 'regime of
psychology minced with moral judgement'.[54]

Most probation officers, if asked to describe what they
do, would explain that they give 'general support' to their
clients and find it hard to be any more specific. Despite a
trend towards exploring different methods of social work to
be practised under probation orders, there is little evidence
of any wholesale adoption and most work is still carried out
on a one-to-one basis.

Permanent Change in the Offender

Although in 'official literature probation is described as a
purposeful activity, in reality it is often characterized by lack
of clarity. Many clients must feel like the juveniles in Giller
and Morris's study, who described supervision as 'boring
and routine' and made such comments as: 'It's just a chore
having to get up and go down there and hang around
waiting', and 'You just go down there for a chat and come
home again. It's a waste of time'.[55] Similarly, the consumers
of probation in the Nottingham survey described probation
as 'a process of aimless talks' and 'a waste of time'.[56]

Probation officers' experience of the exercise often coin-
cides with the description deprecated by Mark Monger: 'a
series of aimless conversations about leisure time activity –
that ancient standby – or visits remarkable for their
brevity'.[57] They sometimes comment jokingly that, although they have asked clients to come into the office, they
don't know why or even what to say to them. Nor is there
evidence of supervision bringing about change in the
offender. Geoffrey Parkinson writes that: 'Caseworkers are
continually bewildered by the continuing delinquencies of

their best clients'.[58] Research has shown that probation is
no more successful in preventing reconviction than other
methods of disposal.

However, we have noted that this is only one aspect of
the change expected. Supervision and casework should
also help clients to come to terms with society and accept
their place in the community. This official aim is at odds
with the intention of many probation officers when deciding to join the probation and after-care service. Geoffrey
Pearson, writing about the generality of social workers,
claims that their choice of work is 'a criticism of the society
in which they live with their clients'.[59]

Few probation officers will have envisaged the job as
tailoring clients to meet the needs of society and few
attempt to do this.

Probation Orders – A Discussion

The probation order has been subject to less critical
examination and analysis than any other major task of the
service. What little is written is dominated by the official
definition and the probation order has even survived the
impact of the radical critique which led to a substantial
re-thinking of most other areas of probation work. Probation officers who have increasingly experienced conflicts in
other tasks have taken refuge in probation as the acceptable
face of their work. The offenders' consent to probation is
seen as a legitimation for involvement, even though any
detached scrutiny casts doubt on the genuineness of that
consent. Probation is welcomed by probation officers as a
non-custodial measure not directly linked to penal institutions. The widespread disregard of formal definitions of
role and of the Probation Rules has made it possible for
probation to be regarded as a professionally directed social
work intervention. For all these reasons probation is seen as
a more acceptable, client-centred activity than other probation tasks and has for the most part escaped criticism.
Nevertheless, we believe that many probation officers
experience the substantial gulf we have described between

official accounts of probation and the practice experience. As with social enquiry reports, there exists a back region account which admits and recognizes these conflicts but which has remained almost totally unarticulated. We now seek to understand the reasons for the conflicts experienced and the disparity between the official account and the real experience.

We have shown that the official account of probation orders describes the process of supervision as a highly specific and ambitious programme aimed at the reformation of the individual offender. It is based on the assumption that the offender's personality, behaviour, attitudes and situation can be changed by the personal influence of the probation officer. Crime is seen as a problem of individual malfunctioning amenable to individual modification via the probation order. This is an extreme example of the *individualized approach to crime,* which has already been outlined with reference to social enquiry reports and which is a fundamental characteristic of the criminal justice system. Probation officers are in practice constrained by this basic approach which creates difficulties in any attempt to treat crime as a socially constructed phenomenon.

Intrinsic to the official probation account is the belief that crime is a maladjusted and pathological response within a sound and just social system. This prompts the search for factors which distinguish 'criminals' from 'normal people'. Once identified these are to be corrected through the probation order which will *reform the individual offender in the image of the law-abiding and responsible citizen.* We have commented on the failure to achieve such transformations in practice. Indeed probation officers have difficulty in discerning clear differences which separate out their clients from other people. Despite these important obstacles the goal of reform continues to underpin probation supervision.

An important feature of the probation order is its duality, combining components of care and control. Much discussion of this has been oversimplified, suggesting that the probation officer exercises care for the benefit of the offender and control for the benefit of the community. This description has allowed the probation officer's role to be viewed in terms of a polarity between care and control. But the official accounts of probation are unambiguous in this connection – they state that the probation officer is to care and control on behalf of the community and both are directed at the offender in the interests of society. It is assumed that *care and control are entirely compatible* and benefit offenders, since both will help offenders to accept their place in society. Indeed it is argued that control is a means of caring; thus the use of control is seen as both justifiable and practicable.

All these asumptions rest on a *consensus view of society:* the offender can only and will only reach fulfilment if in harmony with society. Thus adjustments which can be achieved in this direction will benefit both the offender and the community. If offenders can learn their social duties and comply with society's expectations then they will be content with their lot in life. The whole edifice of probation rests on these unsound foundations. Practical experience contradicts these assumptions at every point – crime is a social construct; in society there are wide divergences of interest which make some peoples' 'lot' less acceptable than others'. For probation officers the issues are not as straight-forward as the official accounts would have us believe. We have described how probation officers repeatedly face difficult choices and are often acutely aware of areas of conflict between the interests of their clients and those of 'society'.

We have described how the job of supervising probation orders is not in practice carried out according to the official definition and indeed it seems clear that there is a degree of official recognition of this disparity. The discretion given to the probation officer in the Probation Rules and the licence they are then given by management to use this discretion liberally indicates that belief in the official account is of more significance than what really happens in practice. We suggest that this can be understood by accepting that the importance of probation must be sought elsewhere than in the material reality of its practice. We identify two ways in which this may be true. First, probation can be said to represent the operation of the liberal state, *the benevolent face of the penal system*. It allegedly gives those who have 'gone astray' a second chance, offering the opportunity of advice, guidance, assistance, befriending, and the chance to take advantage of educational, recreational and social facilities. Yet our account of practice shows that this superficial appearance of probation is at odds with the real experience. But by keeping the official account in the forefront, the penal system is able to maintain its liberal and merciful image.

Secondly, probation orders uphold a set of moral and ethical values which themselves have an *important ideological function and significance*. For instance, they represent to offenders the importance of work, good behaviour, an industrious life, constructive recreational activities, obeying instructions from those in authority and learning from your betters what is good for you. The cumulative and collective impact of these moral imperatives may be significantly greater than their actual effect on any one offender. They represent a set of standards towards which offenders are expected to aspire and which serve particular interests in society. They also legitimate a set of social relations which maintain the status quo and which the offender is expected to accept.

We have now discussed in some detail two important aspects of the probation officer's job. First, we looked at the official accounts and then built up a more realistic picture of the job as it is done, with all its problems and conflicts. Having noted considerable differences between the official account and the way probation officers and clients really operate, we have discussed the reasons for this. The tasks of the probation officer uphold the values of the penal system and indeed support and legitimate those core values and standards which form the ideological base of British society. Yet probation officers are conscious that it is the way this society operates which systematically disadvantages their clients. They face a fundamental contradiction between their aspirations to help and their role. In the next chapter we will examine the prison-based tasks of the probation service, in which this contradiction is also found.

3
Prison-Based Work

We now look at prison welfare and after-care work. These are the probation tasks most closely connected with custodial institutions and both are relatively new, taken on during the rapid expansion of the probation service in the 1960s. We will again contrast the official account with the experience of practice. Space precludes an exhaustive examination of these functions and we will concentrate on identifying the dilemmas encountered by probation officers in their prison-based work.

PRISON WELFARE

The Official Account

Staffing prison welfare departments is a major responsibility of the probation service, with 8–10 per cent of probation officers seconded to prison department establishments at any one time.[1] The Maxwell Report (1953) first recommended that welfare officers be appointed in all prisons to: 'select prisoners wanting, and able to benefit from, personal after-care'. Welfare officers were also to: 'help prisoners during their period of imprisonment . . . to mitigate the numerous difficulties which beset a man or woman whose social ties have been suddenly snapped by a sentence of imprisonment; and by such means establish a relationship of confidence . . . and . . . to prepare constructive after-care plans for their assistance after discharge'.[2] In 1963 the ACTO Report[3] recommended the separate employment of professionally trained social workers in prisons but, despite that recommendation, the probation service assumed responsibility for prison welfare in 1966. A Home Office Circular (1967) laid down the specific duties as follows: 'The seconded officer is a member of the prison team, with the fourfold role of social caseworker, focal point of social work, channel of communications on social problems with the outside world and planner of aftercare'.[4]

The circular modified Maxwell's job description by introducing the task of 'on-going casework with prisoners' and advocating a much closer involvement in the bureaucratic procedures of the prison through, for example, participation in reception, review, home leave and hostel selection boards. More recently, the prison welfare role has been affected by the introduction of parole and the attempt by the probation service to offer after-care to all prisoners. In 1977, it was agreed that prison welfare officers should be renamed prison probation officers. This was only a cosmetic change intended to meet some of the criticism we detail later; here we will use the older, and in our view more accurate title of prison welfare officer.

The fourfold role of the prison welfare officer is seen as complementary to the task of the whole prison, which is said to be the rehabilitation of the prisoner. Jarvis says that:

Despite the welfare officer's primary concern with the welfare of the prisoner and the preparation of his after-care, it must be kept in mind that these matters are the general responsibility of the whole institution and that the welfare officer is a member of a team working to achieve the rehabilitation of the prisoner.[5]

The welfare officer's role is therefore directly linked to official rhetoric about the purpose of prison. Prison Rule No. 1 says that: 'the purpose of the training and treatment of convicted prisoners shall be to encourage them to lead a good and useful life' and Rule No. 3 that: 'at all times the treatment of prisoners shall be such as to encourage their self respect and a sense of personal responsibility'.[6] A

Home Office discussion paper went even further identifying an 'important part of the prison's task as social work
with offenders, using that phrase in its widest sense'; and
arguing that 'the prison service should recognise that
custody should not be seen in isolation. It should be seen as
part of a continuing concern for the offender, or, to use the
current jargon, as part of throughcare.'[7]

The May Report recently echoed the same sentiments
when proposing a new prison rule based on the notion of
'positive custody'.[8] Discussion of the role of the prison
welfare officer clearly cannot be divorced from consideration of the prison system and its declared purpose.

The view of the welfare officer's role contained in professional literature varies little from this official account but
a more critical attitude is taken on the extent to which
prisons actually realize their rehabilitative purpose. Professional accounts urge reform of prisons towards the
rehabilitative ideal and add to the welfare role the task of
humanizing the prisons. Thus reports on prison welfare by
NAPO have called for a 'rehabilitative, treatment-oriented'[9]
prison system and for a 'transformation of the whole prison
system'.[10] The 1976 Report declared: 'we have a contribution to make, not just to individual prisoners but to the
humanising of the institution'.[11] This additional role cannot
be conceded in official accounts because it is based on a
recognition of the inhumane nature of imprisonment.

Another theme in the professional literature is anxiety to
distinguish between what are seen as the mundane welfare
tasks and the practice of social casework, emphasizing the
social work skills of probation officers: 'Welfare is food,
clothing, housing, environment and a sense of well-being
within that environment. Casework deals both technically
and esoterically with the further dimension of the man
within, who in any final analysis is separate and apart from
mere sense appreciation.'[12]

Anxiety to concentrate on casework has produced some
congruence of interests between prison welfare officers and
the Prison Officers Association which, since the early 1960s,
has held a policy of taking on welfare work. This has led to

pilot projects in some prisons in which prison officers develop a welfare role with probation officers acting as social work consultants. Early evidence suggests that these schemes are progressing very slowly and have evoked mixed responses from prison officers and welfare staff.[13]

We have now completed a picture of the official account of the prison welfare role. It can be identified as (1) social casework with prisoners (a task probation officers seek to expand); (2) welfare work with prisoners including communication with the outside world; (3) planning and preparation for release, and (4) minimizing the damage caused by and humanizing the prisons (only found in professional literature). All these specific roles are seen as secondary to an overall role as (5) a member of a prison team engaged in the rehabilitation of the prisoner.

The Practice Account

The authors have not worked in prison welfare posts, so our perspective is that of field probation officers, supplemented by discussion with prison welfare officers and written accounts of this work. The dominant impression is one of enormous variation. Evidence submitted to the 1976 NAPO Report indicated differences in the priorities of various prisons and highlighted the confusion and disparity of approach. The Report noted increasing levels of uncertainty and concluded that: 'probation officers in prisons appear to be doing their own thing as best they can, often with no clear aims in mind and without being very sure where they stand in relation to the prison system or the probation service'.[14]

This provides the general background against which we examine specific aspects of the role.

Social Casework with Prisoners

We have noted that the professional literature stresses the development of a casework approach with prisoners. The content of casework is not precisely defined but the goal is ambitious: 'we see our task not merely in terms of helping individuals but also the introduction into the institutional setting of a much greater opportunity for inmates to live and grow to fuller stature as human beings'. [15]

The critique of social casework which has affected much of social work practice has had little impact on the world of prison welfare.

Although the intention to create opportunities for case-work is clear, much of the literature centres on the difficulties encountered both in principle and in practice. Both NAPO reports dwell on the need for changes in the prison system to provide a suitable environment for case-work: 'the conflict revolves round the difficulty of enabling people to grow and develop in an environment which en-courages dependency and inhibits personal responsibility'. [16]

At a practical level the problems are formidable, par-ticularly in the larger prisons where sheer numbers, rapid turnover and the demands of security are substantial obstacles. Mike Othen complains: 'the work is done at inconvenient times and places, in spare corners, at meal times and after working hours'. [17]

Another theme of discontent is that other prison staff do not see probation officers as caseworkers and seem intent on using them for straightforward welfare tasks or to cool out individual anxiety for the sake of good order. A welfare officer comments: 'where tension has been built up in a prisoner . . . immediate action is requested by the staff to relieve men of anxiety in order to reduce their escape potential'. [18]

Mike Othen argues that such anxiety reduction may interfere with the casework process: 'it is highly question-able from our professional standpoint that that is a desirable aim. It could ultimately be in the client's interests to work through this anxiety'. [19]

Despite these widely acknowledged difficulties in the casework role, proponents of this approach received some support from Shaw's study of prison welfare in Ashwell and Gartree Prisons. [20] An experimental group of prisoners given 'casework' for one hour weekly showed a lower re-conviction rate after two years than a matched control group with normal access to the welfare department. The significance of that finding is reduced by the failure of a similar study by Fowles in Liverpool Prison[21] to produce similar results. A further flaw in the original study was the failure to define the content of the 'casework' received by prisoners.

Welfare Work

Despite their aspirations, prison welfare officers find that their working day more closely resembles Mike Othen's unpretentious description:

> Letters astray, forgotten or crossed; breaking of bad news and coping with feelings aroused; obtaining news of sickness, birth, death; why relative/object of heart's desire has not visited; urgent visits, extra visits; coping and helping to reduce excessive anxiety; parole interviews; commiseration/'be patient my son' interviews in long term establishments: floods of receptions and discharges in others.[22]

Much of the welfare officer's work is dominated by inescapable prison routines. David Smith points out that: 'of the twenty-one functions listed in a Home Office circular of 1967 for the guidance of newly-seconded probation officers, nine had to do with prison management rather than with helping individual prisoners'.[23]

The sheer volume of work arising from the expectation on the welfare officer to contribute to the smooth running of the prison may result in the prisoner's welfare taking second place.

We have commented on the pressure put on the prison welfare officer for immediate action by other staff. Prisoners, too, exert such pressure as John Tracey says: 'there is often a tendency . . . to present problems dramatically to trigger the officer to take the action which the inmate feels is desirable'.[24]

These pressures exist because the prisoner is helpless and the welfare officer has a monopoly over the means of immediate communication with the outside world, the telephone. The welfare officer becomes the channel of communication with the outside world not because that makes for more effective communication but because of prison rules. Mike Othen comments: 'Changing some of these rules . . . would render many of the current welfare tasks superfluous'.[25]

The welfare role is firmly defined and constrained by the discipline and control functions of the prison.

The conflict between the demands of the prison and the needs of the prisoner is made very explicit by Bob Hutchinson in an article about welfare work with politically motivated prisoners:

> Politically motivated prisoners perhaps throw into sharpest focus our continual dilemma of trying to avoid over-identification with one side, and therefore antago-nising the other. . . . If our relationships with uniformed staff are as they should be we shall know where to exer-cise caution, and in cases of doubt, or where we have been previously requested, it is not unusual for us to consult the security officer before carrying out relatively simple tasks such as contacting friends and relatives about their visits.[26]

Clearly the provision of welfare help is not a simple and unambiguous activity for the probation officer in prison.

Planning for Release

The idea that a unique programme of personal after-care could be – and should be – designed for each prisoner, starting from the first day of sentence, forms the basis of the currently fashionable notion of 'through-care'. Bean casts a shadow of reality on the idea, pointing out the huge scale of the task – 60,000 men discharged from prison in 1970 of whom 60 per cent had served sentences of four months or less.[27] The prison welfare records received by probation officers in the field show that prison welfare officers can only cope by being extremely selective and that constructive planning is limited, usually to those serving longer sentences. The 1971 NAPO Report revealed that prison welfare officers had little enthusiasm for the practical aspects of planning for release – clothing and discharge grant applications were seen as work suitable for prison officers.[28]

Provision of clothing for release is often inadequate and even where it is of a good standard many ex-prisoners will discard these reminders of the prison at the first opportunity. The level of discharge grants is woefully inadequate to provide a person with any real sense of security or hope on release. Ex-prisoners are not welcomed back into society and both employment and accommodation are in short supply and are usually sub-standard. These circumstances dictate that only with a small minority of prisoners will prison welfare officers feel that they have formulated any satisfactory plan.

Another block to good planning is that, for a variety of reasons, prisoners are not always truthful about their probable situation on release. Some may falsely claim to be homeless to qualify for the higher rate of discharge grant. Many are affected by the parole system – to secure parole some give addresses where they cannot remain long, or details of jobs which evaporate on release. The main concern of potential parolees is how they can secure early release and to this end they may emphasize only positives and minimize any difficulties. John McVicar claims that: 'parole is extremely corrupting because it sets up prisoners to pretend to be what they're not'.[29]

This will affect relationships with welfare staff – cooperation may be a deliberate strategy to demonstrate maturity and insight in pursuit of a good parole report.

Humanizing the Prisons

There is little evidence that the introduction of probation officers has had any significant effect on prison regimes.

Small successes are claimed in the literature but concern peripheral improvements – for instance in visiting arrangements. A welfare officer commenting on the problems of changing the prison from within, remarks that prison governors: 'although often highly critical about the system . . . do not take kindly to criticisms coming from others'.[30]

It seems particularly arrogant to suppose that the introduction of a few probation officers into a prison will change its nature or protect prisoners from its negative effects. It is more likely that the probation officers will be influenced by the powerful norms of the institution. Implicit in the welfare officer's role is an acceptance of prison rules. It is normally ignored that welfare officers have to accept the role of custodian – equipped with a bunch of keys, they are expected to be no less punctilious than prison officers in ensuring the continued confinement of prisoners behind locked doors. Mike Othen describes the welfare officer's position thus:

The problem for probation officers is not whether we can work in such terrible places but the unpalatable fact that when we do we are part of the dependency-producing, self-respect destroying regime; it is inherent in the various duties we perform on behalf of the institution. The only way of avoiding this would be to tread a path of total conflict with the prison.[31]

Welfare officers are in a weak position to act as safeguards against the worst excesses of the prison system. They are usually kept well away from any trouble in the prison and can be arbitrarily denied normal access to prisoners on the grounds of discipline or security needs. They are often in no position to comment on such matters, even if they wished to do so. Like other prison staff, welfare officers are subject to the Official Secrets Act, a further deterrent. Prison welfare officers have not been prominent in providing the evidence which enables concerned groups to exert pressure for change in the prison system.

Member of the Rehabilitative Prison Team

The official account argues that prison welfare work is just one contribution to the rehabilitation of the prisoner which is the task of the whole prison. Professional accounts are critical of the rehabilitative potential of our present prison system but argue the development of a system geared to rehabilitation. Some cautious notes of optimism are even sounded but hope struggles against an acute awareness of the real state of our prisons. The 1976 NAPO Report points to features of institutional life inimical to rehabilitation: 'the series of rituals, the mores, regulations and sanctions effective from the moment of entry to final departure'.[32]

Phyllida Parsloe tackles the basic issue clearly: 'as anyone who has visited a prison knows, even if it is possible to rehabilitate people compulsorily, and that is at least debatable, the physical and human environment of a prison is not conducive to rehabilitation'.[33]

Probation officers have over the years hoped for improvement, whilst observing the destructive nature of the prison system. By minimizing the negative aspects and promoting the ideal of the therapeutic prison, probation officers have contributed to public mystification about the true nature of our jails. Now, increasingly, probation officers are finding this position intolerable and are prepared to be openly critical of the prisons and to voice the opinion that they cannot be transformed into treatment institutions.

Prison Welfare – A Discussion

We have contrasted the official expectations of the prison welfare officer with some comment on the realities of the job. It is immediately clear that the prison welfare officer plays a *marginal role in the powerful prison system*. Coming from outside with an alien perspective, probation officers are able to exert little influence over other prison staff. The prison welfare officer's task is valued only as long as it contributes to the primary functions of the prison – disci-

pline and control. Ideas about treatment and rehabilitation
are generally accorded low priority and status by other staff
and inmates alike.

The pressures on the prison welfare officer to become
incorporated in the prison regime are very strong, and there is
considerable evidence that this happens. The 1971 NAPO
Reports says: 'it certainly seems that to a large extent
welfare officers have adjusted to the regime within which
they work and would appear to be making every effort to
maintain the even tenor of the system'.[34]

Bob Hutchinson reflects a thorough integration with the
prison system when he says: 'the probation officer working
in prison is not his own master to the extent the field officer
is. We are part of a team within a highly structured situation
whose ultimate responsibility and control do not rest with
us. To be successful we have to integrate and work within
the structure'.[35]

Another fundamental difficulty for prison welfare officers
is that they are charged with mitigating the social problems
caused for a person by a sentence of imprisonment. Most
social work involves, to some degree, an effort to help the
casualties of our social system but a sentence of imprisonment involves the direct punishment of an individual. Any
harm resulting from it is an inherent consequence of
imprisonment and cannot be regarded as an accidental by-
product. It is particularly hypocritical that there should
follow a pretence of caring, of mitigating the damage
intentionally inflicted. Martin Davies describes this afterthought as 'society's apology for the hurt inflicted' and 'an
apology for vengeance'.[36] Given this hypocrisy at the very
root of the welfare role, it is not surprising that some welfare
officers experience the uncomfortable feeling that they are
being used. The provision of a prison welfare service acts as
a sop to the liberal conscience and the major significance of the
role lies elsewhere than in the effectiveness of the help
offered to prisoners.

In the struggle to establish and enlarge the role of probation officers in prison, some of the arguments deployed
have displayed a regrettable arrogance. The probation

service greatly overestimates its potential impact on prisons and is dismissive about the ability, capacity and willingness of prison officers to take on a role wider than the custodian. When a transfer of welfare tasks to prison officers is suggested, this is on the basis that they are too mundane for the skilled probation officer, who should be freed to take up the more grandiose roles of caseworker and consultant.

At the core of the dilemma facing the prison welfare officer lies a question – can the prisons ever develop any substantial rehabilitative function? This is a critical issue because in such a development lies the only hope that the welfare role can ever become a positive one. It is the pressure to formulate a positive role that leads commentators on the development of prison welfare to adopt *an unrealistic and idealistic attitude to the scope for change in the prison system*. The desperation of the reformer shows in the irony of the 1976 NAPO Report when it argues that the changes it wishes to see in the prison system 'are in line with the ideals which Mr Gladstone's Committee enunciated and we feel we are not unduly impatient in wishing those good intentions at last to be translated into actions'.[37] The Gladstone Committee reported in 1894, and it cannot be excessively pessimistic to conclude now that the reason its ideals have not been translated into practice is because they conflict with important functions of prisons in our society.

Against this background it is little wonder that a sharp controversy has developed about the future of probation officers in prisons. The 1976 NAPO Report discusses the uneasy relationship between the probation service and prisons, noting that as experience accumulates the unease increases. Both NAPO reports refer to difficulties experienced in recruiting probation officers to prison welfare posts and this is increasingly an acute problem in many probation areas with coercion being used when promises of promotion fail to attract recruits. Resistance to working in prisons has led to a demand, from within the probation service, for complete withdrawal from prison welfare work. Our analysis of other probation tasks leads us to believe that the conflicts experienced in the prison welfare role are not different in nature from those affecting the field probation officer. The prison welfare role has been the first to be exposed to sustained criticism because the conflicts are experienced at their sharpest in the prison setting.

AFTER-CARE

The Official Account

The term after-care is used to describe a range of tasks involving probation officers in work with men and women during custodial sentences and after release. Here we concentrate on the three major responsibilities of the probation service in this respect – provision of voluntary after-care for any adult prisoner who seeks it; supervision of all young adults (released on licence from Borstals, detention centres and prisons); and supervision of selected adult prisoners released on parole licence. Other after-care responsibilities, such as supervision of those released on licence after serving life sentences or hospital orders, are omitted. The official account holds that all after-care should have a common base and there are strong common elements so we first discuss the general features of after-care. We then look at some differences, particularly between voluntary after-care and statutory licence, and comment on particular issues concerned with parole.

Historically, voluntary and statutory after-care had been carried out by different bodies but the 1963 ACTO Report *The Organisation of After-care*[38] surveyed 'the then existing jungle of after-care provision, some voluntary and some statutory, some provided by voluntary societies and some by various branches of government'.[39] The Report's recommendation that the probation service should assume responsibility for all forms of after-care was implemented in 1965. Parole was introduced in 1968, following the Criminal Justice Act 1967.

The ACTO Report set out four principles regarded as essential to effective after-care:

(1) After-care must be designed to meet the needs both of society and of the individual offenders.

(2) The nature and quality of the after-care service provided should be fundamentally the same and available for all offenders, irrespective of the particular type of sentence which they may have served.

(3) After-care is a form of social work which requires in those undertaking it special qualities of personality and special training and experience.

(4) After-care to be fully effective must be integrated with the work of the penal institutions in which the offender serves his sentence, and must be conceived as a continuing process throughout his sentence and for as long as necessary after release.[40]

The Report develops a definition of the purpose of after-care which Jarvis uses as an official account of the after-care task:

More is required of the community than the provision of material help. While a person about to be discharged from a penal institution needs to have deficiencies in clothing made good and to be given immediate financial aid, these provisions are incidental to the main task. The prime purpose of after-care in the community is to offer the discharged prisoner the friendship, guidance and moral support that he needs if he is to surmount the difficulties that face him in the outside world. Those difficulties are often of a personal or domestic nature; they have sometimes contributed to his former delinquency and may impede his full and lasting social re-adjustment.

Some discharged prisoners need little or no help; for others after-care support during their first few weeks of freedom is sufficient. But many require skilled rehabilitative help for a long time, if a return to prison is to be prevented.[41]

This stresses a shift away from the provision of material

help, which is said to be the function of other state agencies, with the probation service providing a personal social work service. The purpose of this social work help is not merely to deal with difficulties arising from imprisonment, but rather to tackle the problems contributing to the behaviour which led to imprisonment. A close parallel can be seen with the purpose of probation orders – to help offenders accept their place in society and thus make a successful re-adjustment. The official account expresses clearly the belief that in this respect the probation officer is to continue the process of rehabilitation which has been started in the penal institution. Custody and after-care are seen 'as part of a single process, both designed to fit the offender to take his place as a normal member of the community'.[42] This view of after-care as a continuation of rehabilitation, provides the basis from which some practitioners have argued for the use of the term 'through-care'. Help is not to be confined to prisoners but extended to their families who should be assisted with problems arising from the enforced absence of one of the family, and with difficulties experienced on the return. This family work should extend beyond mere welfare concern. The ACTO Report identifies it as an essential part of the rehabilitative effort: 'In many cases domestic troubles have already been present and may indeed have contributed to the commission of the offences' and the probation officer should 'endeavour that the offender returns to better home relationships than prevailed at the time of his conviction'.[43]

The ACTO Report led to the transfer of responsibility for after-care from voluntary bodies to the probation service. However, it commented on 'the concern of many in the community to help the former offender to re-establish himself' and recommended that this benevolence in society towards discharged prisoners could be expressed by voluntary associates working under the direction of probation officers:

The main need of many offenders is for simple encouragement, friendship and human understanding which could be given by sincere and warm-hearted auxiliaries who had sound common sense and the ability to make themselves acceptable to those whom they sought to help.[44]

This retention of a voluntary element is seen as a valuable contribution to the offender's resettlement in the community.

This official account of the general features of after-care covers all the important aspects of voluntary after-care. An important distinguishing feature is that the intended recipient is free to accept or reject contact with the probation service. We now look at the official account of the distinctive features of statutory licences.

Borstal licences were an innovation in penal thinking when they were introduced as an integral part of the 'Borstal training' concept in 1908. In contrast to earlier ticket-of-leave licences, 'its object was not a sort of police control, but to ensure that the boy was placed under the supervision of a Society whose first object was his rehabilitation, and that he should have regard to their directions and advice at the risk of being recalled if he failed to do so'.[45]

Borstal licence has survived unchanged in philosophy to the present day. The licence, like a probation order, contains a series of requirements which are seen as the framework within which rehabilitation can take place. The licensee is required to keep in touch with the probation officer, to be of good behaviour, to lead an industrious life and to obtain approval for any change of address or employment. Failure to comply with these requirements can result in a recall to Borstal for a period of up to six months; the recall decision is taken through a bureaucratic process for which the Home Secretary is nominally responsible.

Official accounts of 'positive licence' share much with the description of probation given earlier. Again it is assumed that care and control can be combined in a process which meets the needs of the offender and society. The ACTO Report echoes the Morison Report's description of probation:

a society which cherishes responsible freedom also needs to secure its own protection by means which nevertheless minimise the restrictions necessarily imposed on the offender. Supervised liberty, in the form of compulsory after-care supervision for appropriate offenders, is therefore seen as an alternative to some extent to their continued segregation from the community in penal institutions, with all the economic and social disadvantages which that entails.[46]

The Criminal Justice Act 1961, extended 'positive licence' to young prisoners (under 21 at date of sentence) and those released from detention centres. These two more recent types of licence for young offenders were based on the Borstal licence, contain similar requirements and are not usually distinguished from them in official accounts.

Finally, parole licence must be differentiated from those already discussed because it is not automatic. Available to adult prisoners serving sentences over 18 months it is described as: 'a state which a prisoner can earn'.[47] Parole is based on a theory of peak response to imprisonment. The White Paper (1965) which preceded its introduction stated:

What is proposed is that a prisoner's date of release should be largely dependent on his response to training and his likely behaviour on release. A considerable number of long-term prisoners reach a recognisable peak in their training at which they may respond to generous treatment, but after which, if kept in prison, they may go downhill. To give such prisoners the opportunity of supervised freedom at the right moment may be decisive in securing their return to decent citizenship.[48]

Parole too is clearly based on a rehabilitative model with the helping process backed by sanctions. The general requirements resemble those of other licences, although special requirements covering a wide range of controls may be added. Probation officers are expected to exercise parole

licences strictly and should notify the Home Secretary
(following the correct bureaucratic procedures):

> not only in any case where contact with a licensee is lost,
> a condition has been broken, or there has been another
> change but also where there is anything in the offender's
> response, situation or behaviour that presents an actual
> or potential risk to the public, that seems likely to bring
> the parole scheme into disrepute, or that may make it
> necessary to consider recall.[49]

Jarvis writes that: 'the supervising officer is entitled to
expect a conscientious regard for the conditions of the
licence, for reporting instructions and for advice
generally'.[50]

There have been relatively few professional accounts of
after-care work; those that have appeared have differed
little from the official account and have been mainly concerned with practical issues. There has been discussion
about the organization of after-care work and in particular
the creation of specialized after-care units in the major
urban centres. Another focus for discussion has been pre-
release work, and the use of letter-writing and group work
as means of developing useful relationships with clients in
institutions. Perhaps the most significant theme implicit in
the literature, and reflected in the practice of some probation services, is an emphasis on 'through-care'. This
seeks to build on the ideas of rehabilitation and continuity
of treatment which feature in the official account.

After-care arrangements for young adults have been the
subject of extensive debate in recent years. The Younger
Report (1974)[51] proposed a 'custody and control' sentence,
combining an indeterminate period in custody with a complementary period of 'control in the community' under a
stricter and significantly strengthened licence. There was
strong resistance to these proposals from NAPO. With attention focused on statutory after-care, criticism of existing
arrangements increased, leading to calls within the association for the abandonment of all compulsory after-care,

including parole. Although these have never gained majority support, the debate continues.

The subsequent Green Paper (1978)[52] abandoned much of the earlier report but retained the proposal for stronger licences. With a change of government, the recent White Paper *Young Offenders* (1980)[53] appears to have settled for a continuation of licences in their existing form but with their length reduced. The paper proposes a major change in recall arrangements, proposing that both breaches of conditions and further offences should be dealt with by the courts. Borstals are to be merged with other young prisoner institutions in a 'youth custody' stystem. Legislation on these proposals now seems imminent, producing some superficial change in the arrangements we have outlined.

We have now completed our discussion of the official account of after-care and can identify the main components of after-care as (1) a personal social work service, intended (2) to continue the rehabilitative process begun in the institution and aimed at dealing with the problems which led to imprisonment. There is (3) a growing tendency to call this process through-care. (4) Help is extended to the family as well as the prisoner and (5) the concern of the community is represented by the involvement of voluntary associates. Particular aspects needing attention are (6) the freedom of prisoners to accept or reject voluntary after-care, (7) the attempt to combine help with sanctions in 'positive licences' and (8) the special nature of parole.

The Practice Account

Before examining these features of the official account some general points should be made. After-care has grown rapidly to become one of the probation service's major tasks but, despite fears that it is taking over, it still tends to be the poor relation amongst the service's work with voluntary after-care especially vulnerable to cut-backs. The Home Office NARS Study showed that most of the time spent on after-care went on statutory licences with voluntary work taking up only about 4 per cent of the probation service's time. Despite the attention it attracts, parole accounts for only about 2 per cent of the service's time.[54]

Practical problems make pre-release work a time-consuming and frustrating activity. Most probation officers believe there is no substitute for visits if any real link is to be made with a prisoner, but these are the first victims of economy in the service. Visits need to be fitted into the prison's rigidly defined hours and poor facilities, combined with the oppressive institutional atmosphere, prevent relaxed and constructive interviews. Usually welcomed by prisoners, at the very least they provide an opportunity for a good smoke and a break in the monotony of prison routine. Their purpose is often less than clear – although most prisoners identify material assistance as their primary after-care need, they recognize that little practical help is on offer. Probation officers share an awareness of this limitation and are often self-consciously offering only a 'relationship', the purpose of which may be clear to neither party.

This hesitant uncertainty of purpose continues to characterize the work of probation officers with prisoners following release. Although the trauma of release from the total institution is well documented, the probation service makes little effort to intervene on the day of release. The ambiguity of the relationship with the prisoner makes it unlikely that such intervention would be welcome in most cases. Post-release after-care and supervision of licences is quickly absorbed into the probation officer's routine. People are seen on busy reporting evenings; licensees who fail their appointments are chased but with less enthusiasm than probationers.

A Personal Social Work Service

The official account emphasizes that the probation service should provide a personal social work service rather than material aid, which, it is argued, is the function of other state agencies. However, any objective appraisal of the material aid given to prisoners on discharge must conclude that virtually nothing is done to assist their resettlement in the community. We have already commented on how help given by the prison, for instance with clothing, is rejected by many released prisoners. The so-called discharge grant is not even a grant at all now, but an advance payment of social security benefit entitlement. Accommodation facilities for the released prisoner are limited, inevitably second-rate and often offered in a way which is unaccept-able. Released from the restrictive prison environment ex-prisoners are likely to want accommodation with no strings attached, rather than the rules, regulations and interference which they encounter in hostels. The availability of accom-modation on the private market is shrinking and, even under new legislation, housing authorities largely ignore the housing needs of the homeless ex-prisoner. Nor is there any state provision to help ex-prisoners compete for suit-able employment. A model for after-care based on the notion that other state agencies meet material needs is unrealistic.

More in hope than expectation, prisoners continue to ask probation officers who offer help for 'somewhere decent to live and a reasonable job'. Although the official account suggests that the probation service should not be involved in giving material aid, the evidence suggests that in practice the situation is different. A Home Office research project on the work of after-care units demonstrated that clients generally came to the units with pressing material needs: 'after-care units were functioning as second order welfare agencies distributing clothing and money and dealing with employment and accommodation problems. The after-care units were, in effect, supplementing the assistance which clients had from the general social security system'.[55]

Although that research was published in 1971, little has changed since and most probation officers will recognize that description. If anything, the trend is towards greater practical provision in recognition of the demands pre-sented. The probation service is becoming more involved in the provision of after-care hostels (some now providing unstaffed bedsit accommodation) and day centre facilities. Perhaps the main development has been in employment and accommodation advice schemes, although these have struggled to move beyond the provision of information about low-paid, low-grade jobs and sub-standard lodging house accommodation.

Even by extending material provision the probation service has made little impact. Martin Davies understates the position when he says: 'there is a recognisable gap between the needs which ex-prisoners perceive as being primary and the resources which the social aid agencies in general and the probation service in particular have at their disposal'.[56] The more esoteric role of providing personal care through a social work service is on the whole rejected by ex-prisoners. After-care work has to concentrate on material aid and is not only a second-order welfare service but also a second-rate one.

A Continuation of Rehabilitation

The official account assumes that a process of rehabilitation goes on within prisons and other custodial institutions – pre-release work is seen as a contribution to that process and after-care an essential continuation of it. In discussing prison welfare we rejected that picture of prison and need not labour that point here. The London Branch of NAPO in response to the Younger Report commented:

> We think that the experience of institutionalisation is deleterious in almost every case, and our experience in this respect is supported by modern sociological research. The damage to the individual caused by a custodial sentence for most people outweighs any advantage which might accrue from any programme of training.[57]

Prisoners, too, reject the concept of rehabilitative incarceration. Martin Davies, reviewing prisoners' autobiographies, comments that:

> The bitterest and most telling denunciations are against those members of the penal establishment who claim . . .

that custodial sentences are achieving positive ends, by virtue of education and training, welfare and casework, therapy and good advice.[58]

Shorn of the element of continuity, the idea that the focus of social work in after-care should be resolution of the problems which led to imprisonment can carry little conviction. This concept of after-care has close parallels with the official objectives of the probation order. Many of our comments on the practice of probation apply equally here and casework in after-care faces additional hazards. During a prisoner's sentence, the practical problems we have mentioned, combined with the powerful and unreal setting of the prison, prevent realistic work on the problems to be faced outside. As we have already pointed out, after release material problems predominate. This whole approach rests on an individualized view of crime, which locates the reason for the client's imprisonment in personal inadequacy – a perspective which many probation officers and most clients would reject.

The experience of practice leads probation officers to a more humble view of the after-care role. We agree with Martin Davies when he says:

so far as most prisoners are concerned . . . the efforts of the probation officer may be directed almost wholly at helping the ex-offender to overcome the negative effects of his recent conviction – to rehabilitate him as much from the effects of the custodial experience as from the repercussions of his own behaviour.[59]

We believe that probation officers persist in their after-care work because they: 'wish to provide something for the prisoner to make good the damage done',[60] but are acutely aware of the inadequacy of what they can offer.

The Growth of 'Through-Care'

Through-care assumes a rehabilitative regime in the prison and a continuity between 'treatment' in custody and 'treatment' in the community. Neither of these conditions is met in the reality of prison regimes and after-care provision. There are also formidable practical hurdles to be faced if the probation service was seriously considering adoption of a through-care approach. The large number of people sentenced to imprisonment each year (73,000 in England and Wales in 1978) virtually precludes this. The impact on a prisoner's experience of prison which could be made by a few visits (even if cuts allowed them) will be minimal. Long-sentence prisoners would face a long series of through-carers as the mobility of the social work profession took its toll.

In most areas 'through-care' is talked about rather than really attempted. Probation officers use the term to describe an approach far from the original meaning. For most people, through-care means little more than making a link with a prisoner before release in order to have some foundation for work on discharge. More consistent links may be kept in a relatively few cases where existing clients receive sentences of imprisonment. 'Through-care' is already a decayed concept and that may be just as well, for any attempt at systematic 'through-care' is likely simply to divert resources from a more realistic provision of after-care services.

Help to the Family

The official account extends help to the family because family problems may have caused the offence leading to imprisonment. Most attention centres on 'prisoners' wives' but probation officers may have to deal with other family members. They are, for instance, expected to work with the parents of Borstal inmates in the hope of improving the home environment. These attempts are often unwelcome because parents do not generally see their children's offences as caused by problems in the home: 'S/he did the stealing, not us' is a typical response to attempts at family work. Probation officers often find themselves pressing a reluctant family to accept their son or daughter home simply because no alternative accommodation can be found.

Most family work undertaken by the probation service involves contact with women (married or not) left to cope with children by the imprisonment of their partner. Such women are persistently called 'prisoners' wives' or 'mums' instead of being recognized as individuals. Martin Davies recognizes that there are some special problems related to the stigma of prison but comments that: 'many of the problems are similar to those of all one parent families . . . one cannot but feel . . . that material needs must be first and foremost in the minds of most prisoners' wives'.[61]

Not surprisingly, probation officers again find themselves being asked for material aid in an area where their resources are extremely limited, although necessary help can be offered to inexperienced women to ensure that they receive their meagre welfare benefits entitlement. The probation service's more ambitious attempts at emotional support, relationship counselling and teaching 'good mothering' struggle against this predominance of poverty.

The concerns of prisoners and their families do not always coincide and the probation officer can experience acute moral dilemmas about whose interests should prevail. It is not unusual to find a woman considering divorce or some other move towards independence while her partner is in prison. The probation officer may agree that this is right for her, although clearly against the interests of the defined client, the prisoner. A variant of the same dilemma may arise when a prisoner encourages the probation officer to visit his partner, 'to keep an eye on her', with the implicit expectation that the officer will see off any competition and report back on any indiscretions. The official account ignores such problems and assumes a neat congruence of interests which rarely exists in practice.

The Involvement of Voluntary Associates

The official account argues that society has an interest in the re-integration of offenders and that representatives of the community acting in a voluntary capacity can aid the process of resettlement. Discharged prisoners face discrimination, both formal and informal, in the job and housing markets, dependent only upon a miserly discharge grant. This material provision is a better representation of society's real attitude than the proffered friendship of a well-meaning volunteer which, in that context, seems a pale shadow of a welcome-back into society.

Nor is the practical experience in the use of volunteers entirely successful. Phyllida Parsloe points to two problems encountered by attempts to use volunteers: 'Not only do trained social workers have, at best, mixed feelings towards volunteers, but the voluntary associates themselves had difficulties in finding acceptable and appropriate ways of offering help to former prisoners'.[62] Prisoners are often suspicious of the motives of associates and initial meetings between the two can be stilted, artificial encounters. Studies have indicated a high rate of breakdown because the offender rejects the relationship. Voluntary associates, are by no means 'representatives' of the community and many probation officers would recognize Martin Davies's description that they 'represent would-be social workers or self-perceived social leaders rather than the originally conceived man in the street'.[63] The probation service's use of volunteers has been fraught with difficulties, although some slow progress may be made as volunteers have started to organize themselves to provide services through social clubs, literacy schemes and other similar ventures.

Voluntary After-Care

The distinguishing feature of voluntary after-care is that the prisoner is free to accept or reject the attention of the probation officer. This element presents some problems, because probation officers are used to working with clients constrained, to a greater or lesser extent, to maintain contact. The voluntary relationship places the officer under greater pressure to deliver a useful and relevant service to the client if contact is to be maintained. Some element of voluntarism has now been removed from pre-release contacts by the introduction of the parole system. Any prisoner serving over 18 months is likely to accept and encourage attention from a probation officer during the sentence because that is widely believed to increase parole chances.

In practice voluntary after-care suffers from poor take-up. Case-load figures clearly indicate that while more contacts are being made, particularly pre-release, prisoners do not generally keep in touch after discharge. Phyllida Parsloe comments that: 'The majority of voluntary after-care contacts are either single interviews or extend far less than one month'.[64] This is perhaps not surprising in view of the limited help available and the disparity we have already noted between what after-care clients want and what is usually on offer.

Positive Licences

Borstal, detention centre and young prisoners' licences are officially portrayed as an opportunity for help and advice to be given to young people on release, their cooperation being secured by the threat of recall. In practice, these licences are viewed as anything but positive by their subjects – they are bitterly resented as a form of double-sentencing and an unwelcome reminder of the institution. Bottoms and McClintock's study of Borstal inmates showed that fewer than half expected to obtain benefit from after-care supervision, fewer than a quarter saw their probation officer as much as fortnightly and more than two-thirds were assessed by their probation officers as either unco-operative or only passively cooperative.[65] This combination of resentment, low expectations and poor response corresponds with the everyday experience of probation officers. Most licensees have a realistic attitude to the sanction of recall. A client colourfully captured the futility of the licence by describing it to one of the authors as 'like having a fly on your back'.

Probation officers often share much of this perspective and use their discretion to permit infrequent reporting. The examination of the Younger Report by the London Branch of NAPO points out how little recall is used as a sanction: 'In 1972 only twenty-seven orders of recall to dentention centre were issued . . . [and] only fifty-six borstal re-call orders were issued for breach of licence conditions' and argues that: 'Probation officers are clearly reluctant to have someone who has been in no further trouble with the law returned to detention centre . . . or to borstal'.[66]

As with voluntary after-care, probation officers may have doubts about the quality of help they can offer but licences contain additional problems. In contradiction to the helping role, when a client fails to cooperate the probation officer is expected to initiate proceedings perceived to be directly contrary to the client's interests. The London Branch document points out: 'the confusion arising from combining care and control in a single process'.[67] We have already noted the problems experienced in supervising probation orders and these are, if anything, intensified in the supervision of licences.

Parole

The special features of parole contained in official accounts are its reliance on the peak performance theory and the requirement that it should be a stricter and more intensive form of supervision. The idea of a peak response to custody rests heavily on the assumption that prisons are performing a rehabilitative role. We have already argued at length that this is not true and that most probation officers recognize this in their practice. Nor does the process of parole selection pay any great heed to the peak theory on which it is based. The release decision may depend more upon the prisoner's computer-predicted prospects of re-offending than any appraisal of response to the prison regime. As Martin Davies points out: 'The basic selection for parole, however rational it may appear in the eyes of the Parole Board, the local Review Committee, the Home Office or external observers, is unlikely to coincide with the prisoner's view of fair play'.[68] Probation officers are onlookers in the selection process, often puzzled by apparently inconsistent decisions and convinced that the original offence carries as much weight in the selection process as individual characteristics of the prisoner.

On release, parolees tend to regard the licence as a necessary evil to be endured, the price for early release. Robin Parker and Brian Williams's study of parolees showed that they 'report promptly, ask for no help and evade discussion of areas of tension' and that 'problems [were] only revealed after the parole period ended'.[69]

As with other statutory after-care, the probation officer's power to instigate recall is unlikely to encourage the sort of therapeutic discussion envisaged by the official account. Phyllida Parsloe comments: 'the fact that supervising officers have the power to instigate recall . . . makes it impossible for some offenders and difficult for many others to see them as helpful or trustworthy people'.[70] Before or after release, parole can lay claim to little therapeutic or rehabilitative purpose.

More explicitly than any other probation task, parole is portrayed as an attempt to control behaviour but the official expectation of greater strictness and more intensive supervision is not realized in practice. Phyllida Parsloe points out that 'in theory, supervising officers are required to report any breaches of the conditions of the licence. In fact it is well known that they exercise considerable discretion'.[71] In practice, probation officers tend to deal with parole cases in the same way as other types of supervision. The Home Office NARS Study provides the most recent evidence that contact with parolees was on average no more intensive than that with probationers, about two hours per month.[72] The official expectation that parolees will be closely monitored is certainly not achieved in practice. Most probation officers would not even regard it as an appropriate aim, as truly effective monitoring would require the abandonment of a social work approach in favour of more effective surveillance techniques.

After-Care – A Discussion

This account of after-care has indicated many points in common with the other main tasks of the probation service, particularly prison welfare and supervision of probation orders. Our discussion here will reflect these similarities and, coming last, will highlight some of the basic conflicts and contradictions which run through all probation work, although they may be experienced in differing forms in the various tasks.

In common with prison welfare work, we have shown that the official account of after-care is firmly grounded in *the false notion that custodial institutions can be rehabilitative.* The system of after-care is built on the belief that rehabilitation begins in the prison, that 'through-care' visits reinforce the process and make it possible for the probation officer to complete this reformation following the prisoner's release. Most probation officers reject this and regard the prisons, detention centres and Borstals they visit as negative, damaging places. This criticism is often muffled, however, because, like their prison welfare colleagues, officers in the field are inclined to espouse unrealistic and idealistic hopes for change in the prison system. The position of the after-care officer is even more marginal than that of the prison welfare officer, so the limits of personal impact on the prison are more clearly recognized. Probation officers' muted criticism of the prisons is an obstacle to attempts to expose their true nature and helps to mask the negative reality of custodial institutions. Proposals for positive transformations of the prison system help to deflect attention from the need for real change. Martin Davies eloquently describes the issue which probation officers face:

The unique quality of twentieth-century prisons compared with other total institutions is the almost wholly negative profile that they present to their inmates – no matter what the prison administration may intend, no matter what the hopes and aspirations of those intimately involved may be . . . they each participate in, and contribute to, the perpetuation of one of Britain's more corrupting social institutions.[73]

Leaving aside the basic belief in a continuous rehabilitative process, after-care is intended to provide a personal social work service with the aim of *reforming the individual offender*. Here we can see close parallels with the probation order and the analytical points we made in that connection apply equally here. The aim of reformation is based upon an individualized approach to crime and a view of the criminal act as a maladaptive piece of pathological behaviour. No attention is given to crime as a social phenomena or the criminal as a social construction.

After-care, like probation, is based upon *a consensus view of society* in which everyone has an equal chance. Voluntary after-care, no less than statutory after-care, is exercised on behalf of the community with the intention of fitting ex-prisoners to take their places in society and to comply with its demands. Those misguided enough to break the rules must be excluded from society; but when they have been punished and the time comes for their release, help and guidance are available. Probation officers are employed to act as representatives of the caring community, and assisted by unpaid voluntary associates are to extend this conditional welcome back – ex-offenders who have learned the lesson can be totally rehabilitated. The consensus view admits no recognition of the injustice, inequality, discrimination and poverty endemic in our society.

After-care licences are all based, like probation orders, on *the assumption that care and control are entirely compatible*. The prisoner's good behaviour following release is to be ensured by a combination of help from the probation service and the threat of recall for non-compliance. We have argued that the intention of after-care is unambiguously to meet the requirements of society; the intention of control sanctions is overtly stated to be a reassurance to the public that its interests are being safeguarded. We have shown that the controls can interfere with the ability to help and affect the way in which the offer of help is viewed. This duality poses sharp conflicts for probation officers in practice.

In our account of practice we have indicated that many probation officers reject the front-region account of after-care as a rehabilitative process. A back-region account of after-care as simply trying to help the casualties of the prison system exists and is sometimes openly stated. Even where this view receives some official support within a probation area, the service is largely confined to the methods of the rehabilitative/reformative approach; the individual relationship is proffered rather than a range of realistic services designed to meet the problems actually presented by ex-prisoners.

Even this more limited view of after-care presents problems for probation officers. In our discussion of prison welfare we identified the problems associated with acting as 'society's apology for the hurt inflicted'. In the same way, dealing with the casualties of the prison system acts as a reassurance that prisoners are receiving expert (and therefore adequate) help in overcoming the distress and difficulties arising from imprisonment. This sop to the liberal conscience helps to assuage doubts about the use of imprisonment and to deflect any real scrutiny. As with prison welfare, after-care officers are asked to deal with problems which are a direct result of the deliberate imposition of incarceration, not an accidental by-product. As probation officers watch their clients being sentenced to imprisonment when they have suggested an alternative, it is not surprising that they become depressed with *the futility of acting as an apology for hurt inflicted*.

4
New Developments

The four major tasks we have examined still form the basis of probation work but the past few years have been a time of rapid change in the probation service. The new developments are significant, not only because of the time and resources they employ, but also because they indicate how the work of the service is evolving. Rather than select a few for detailed study, our aim is to present a general picture of the range of changes taking place. We look first at developments resulting from legislative changes and then at those arising from initiatives within the service. Drawing the two strands together, we explore the relationship between these new developments and traditional work, identify some issues raised by them and consider their effect on the role of the probation service.

NEW TASKS IN LEGISLATION

These tasks all arose from the Criminal Justice Act 1972, legislation which included: 'a range of new provisions designed to strengthen and extend the powers of courts to deal with offenders'.[1] Of importance to the probation service were provisions for community service, day training centres, probation hostels and bail hostels.

Community service is by far the most significant recent development in the probation service, this was first recommended in the Wootton Report[2] and in 1972 introduced as an 'alternative to imprisonment'. Its main features are outlined in *A Guide for the Courts*, which says the Act gives:

72

the courts power to order offenders to carry out unpaid work of service to the community during their spare time, up to a maximum of 240 hours. . . . The provision is envisaged as a means of imposing the sanction of deprivation of leisure for a constructive and outward looking purpose which will enable the offender to give something back to the community against which he has offended and will in some cases bring him into direct contact with members of the community who most need help and support. . . . The Government has aimed at providing a power which the courts and public will see as a viable alternative to the shorter custodial sentence.[3]

Since its experimental introduction in six areas, it has been rapidly extended to all parts of the country. The number of orders made has grown, from 1,213 in 1974 to 12,782 in the 12 months ending March 1978.[4] This growth has made community service an increasingly significant part of the service's work. Special community service units have been created in most probation areas, involving more clerical and ancillary staff than other work. The units' duties include finding appropriate unpaid work, ensuring that offenders carry it out and taking breach action against those who fail to cooperate. The work carried out by offenders is normally practical, manual labour though in a wide range of settings from old peoples' homes to canal restoration.

From the start, the philosophy of community service has been confused and ambiguous, seeking to combine elements of punishment, atonement, reparation and rehabilitation. Most interest groups could find their aims represented in this penal measure and this has contributed to its wide appeal. This early popularity means that it has not yet been subject to serious evaluative study. It has involved the probation service more clearly and directly than before in the administration of a punishment. Paradoxically the search for work projects and work supervisors has brought the service into closer contact with community groups, although the separate organization of community service has limited the benefits thus gained. One immediate cause for concern is that, although introduced as an 'alternative to custody', experience and some evidence suggests that already it is used primarily where a sentence of imprisonment would not have been imposed. Another concern is the high proportion of unemployed offenders engaged in community service work, particularly in the light of current sensitivity about the relationship between paid and unpaid labour.

Four *day training centres* were set up on an experimental basis as a result of the 1972 Act. But unlike community service, there has not been any extension of this experiment. Intended as another non-custodial alternative, day training centres were to provide 'full time non-residential training for offenders with the aim of equipping them to cope more adequately with the normal demands of modern life' for the 'inadequate recidivist whose offences often reflect a lack of basic skills and tend to lead to a succession of short custodial sentences which usually afford little opportunity for the kind of training from which he might benefit'.[5]

Attendance at a day training centre is on a full-time basis for 60 days and is a condition of a probation order. Each centre operates a different regime, varying from the 'social skills training' focus in Sheffield to the concentration on personal relationships 'through intensive work in small therapeutic groups' in London.[6] Considerable emphasis is placed on a return to the job market at the end of 60 days, and appropriate leisure activities are encouraged. The high cost of day training centres seems a major factor preventing future extension of such facilities.

The 1972 Criminal Justice Act empowered probation and after-care committees for the first time to establish their own *probation hostels* for 'the rehabilitation of offenders'[7] to add to the existing probation hostels managed by voluntary organizations. Although the number of hostels remains quite small, it doubled between 1972 and 1978 and the majority are now managed by probation committees rather than the voluntary sector. An official definition of their purpose says:

Probation hostels which are managed by the service or voluntary organisations provide some supervision and control and the residents can be helped with their personal problems, learn acceptable social behaviour, and acquire the habits of regular work and the ability to make good use of leisure.[8]

Offenders are sent to probation hostels as a condition of a probation order. Regimes vary considerably: some try to replicate a family atmosphere; some are more 'institutional' with communal eating facilities and rather sparse dormitories; others run on a single room, self-catering basis designed to encourage self-reliance and independence.

Allied to this growth of probation hostels has been the growth of *bail hostels*, an innovatory provision 'for persons who would otherwise be remanded in custody because they have no fixed address'.[9] Some probation hostels contain 'bail beds' reserved for this purpose. The provision of bail hostels involves two significant developments in the role of the probation service. It extends its area of concern into pre-trial work with unconvicted defendants and involves a clear assumption of the 'custodian role', with a duty to report breaches of rules or absconding to the police.

SERVICE INITIATIVES

Behind many of the changes initiated from within the service has been the desire to introduce a range of methods and facilities more relevant and successful than traditional one-to-one casework. 'Differential treatment' has been the theme. Additionally, probation officers have increasingly felt compelled to provide 'alternatives to imprisonment', tailored to the requirement to be 'realistic and credible' with the courts. New schemes and projects have sprung up in an uncoordinated way: many of them are undocumented; few are monitored; and while some thrive others 'fade away' or are axed. In surveying the range of projects we have been largely dependent on their own written accounts, an approach with obvious limitations. We hope our first-hand experience of a number of them has allowed a realistic use of this material, highlighting the developments which appear most significant.

Day centres are one of the most popular and fast-expanding new provisions. Elizabeth Burney wrote that in late 1979 centres were being opened at the rate of about one a month.[10] They have been acknowledged by the Home Office as an important area of future expansion, particularly in dealing with the petty persistent offender.[11] Existing day centres range from elaborately established, well-docu-mented prestige projects to small local experiments using existing staff and premises. There seems to be almost as many variations in style and regime as there are centres. At one extreme, for example, is the Wayside Project in Newcastle where the baseline aim is to provide 'somewhere to go – someone to talk to'.[12] It operates as a casual drop-in centre providing simple shelter, physical comfort and referral on to other specialist agencies when necessary. At the other extreme are the day centres with structured regimes and definite programmes (not unlike day training centres) such as those at Leicester, Gillingham and Pontefract.[13] Such centres claim to provide an 'alternative to imprisonment' – clients attend as a condition of their pro-bation order, strict attendance requirements are backed by the threat of breach and regimes tend to be specifically employment focused. Other day centre provision lies somewhere between these two extremes. At the Barbican Centre, for example, attendance is voluntary and contact can remain on a casual basis. But the declared purposes of the project are to help towards change those whose lives exhibit personal or social inadequacy and to break into cyclical patterns of failure by providing social supports, education, personal and social skills. To become a member of the project the client must enter into a contract with the centre staff, thus expressing firm commitment to change.[14]

Accommodation and employment projects are examples of the probation service's move towards more practical provision in recognition of client need. Accommodation schemes are not extensively documented but range from referral and landlady schemes to actual provision of accommodation. We have already commented on our experience of the limited success of landlady and referral schemes, arising from the difficulty of competing on the open market for limited and inadequate provision. In some areas the probation service has, on its own initiative, or in cooperation with a housing association, provided bedsit schemes for single homeless offenders, though these can barely scratch the surface of an enormous unmet need. A more ambitious development is 'the constellation experiment' initiated by the Home Office in 1974–5. Designed to provide a framework within which the probation service and voluntary agencies would survey existing accommodation for offenders, work together to make the best use of them and, when appropriate, develop resources to cover unmet need, [15] these experiments have received further encouragement recently. [16]

There is similarly a wide range of employment projects, from job-placement schemes to training programmes and direct provision of work experience. Job-placement services are on the increase – in October 1978 Roy Bailey identified 11 well-established schemes[17] and it is probable that more now exist. Their purpose is to provide a job-placement service specifically for probation clients, through cultivation of contacts with local employment offices and employers. Employment training schemes work on a day centre basis and aim to 'equip clients with the knowledge and skills to find work for themselves and maintain themselves in it'. The same workshop programme identifies what clients need to learn: 'the acceptance of authority, dealing with frustration and finding satisfaction in relatively mundane work'. [18] The focus of these workshops is on equipping offenders to compete in the labour market. Regimes and the degree of compulsion vary but at least one has a large proportion of clients attending as a condition of probation. [19]

Other projects concentrate on providing work for offenders, mostly as a preparation for joining the labour market. Inner London's Bulldog Project, modelled on New

York's Wildcat Scheme, is in fact a limited company aiming:

> to concentrate on solving one problem: that of unem-
> ployability, by creating a realistic work situation in which
> regular and graded demands are made upon employees.
> The demands are intended to secure regular attendance,
> to improve performance and to engender a more realistic
> and reasonable attitude to authority at the work site. For
> employees there is also a clear objective – placement in
> more remunerative work outside of Bulldog.[20]

Efforts are made to simulate a real work situation. The
work undertaken includes painting and decorating, reno-
vation, cleaning, gardening, concreting and fencing.
Bulldog workers are paid a wage thought to be adequate but
designed to be less than they would receive on the open
labour market. Other probation areas have been involved in
different ways in the Manpower Services Commission Job
Creation Projects for youth, designed to offer limited work
experience to the unemployed.[21] These ventures are likely
to continue expanding unless the MSC budget for such
schemes is severely pruned. It is ironic that the probation
service's involvement in employment projects is rapidly
expanding precisely at the time when recession is severely
reducing job opportunities.

Many *new methods* of social work with offenders have
been promoted and adopted on a limited basis. Some
examples of these new approaches are group work, family
therapy, social skills training, task-centred social work,
detached work and welfare rights work. Impetus for this
development came from the Impact Experiment which,
although failing to produce evidence that intensive supervision necessarily benefited clients or reduced crime, did
seem to show a 'differential effect' – the right treatment
needed to be applied to the appropriate client.[22] This
furthered the use of methods introduced into the probation
service during the experiment and legitimated the search
for an expanded range of social work methods. Space pre-

cludes a fuller examination of all these new approaches so we concentrate on two: group work and social skills.

Although group work is often referred to as a new method, it has been practised in various forms for many years, though there have been fresh initiatives recently. It covers a range of activities, the main feature being that clients of the same type, or thought to have similar problems, are brought together for a common purpose: group therapy (comparatively rare in the probation service), discussion, or to take part in some activity. Client groupings thought appropriate have included sex offenders, adolescents, Borstal trainees, the unemployed, social isolates and 'prisoners' wives'. Activity groups for younger clients are particularly popular. Some examples from descriptions of groups run by probation officers give an idea of the purpose and function of the groups:

Unemployed groups are designed to assist all age groups in finding work and also to help cope with the frustrations of unemployment.[23]

The group of mothers attending the centre is divided into two so that each mother attends the sewing and craft classes one morning each week and the home economics class on the other morning. Cooking tuition aims to help with budgeting for and cooking inexpensive meals, with emphasis on balanced nutrition and the tutor also teaches other basic skills needed to cope with a home and family.[24]

The offenders involved meet weekly as a group with the probation officer running the scheme. The object of this group meeting is to internalise the need for regular taking of the drug, to examine guilt and to help the offender gain insight[25] (sex offenders' group).

The primary objective has been to provide an opportunity for adventure, excitement and a sense of achievement and to give boys an experience of working

together as a group in the company of an adult male[26]
(Scunthorpe cycling group).

Despite extensive promotion over many years, groupwork
remains a minority activity in the probation service.

Social skills training is the latest social work fashion
enjoying increasing popularity. It has been enthusiastically
advocated by its British promoters as a new, straightforward approach – an alternative to the 'second class
service' they claim is now provided by social workers.[27]
Social skills training aims to help people solve immediate
problems, improve their ability to cope with future
problems and to develop better ways of achieving those
goals.[28] Its attractiveness lies in its concentration on
immediate issues, its claim of general applicability, the
opportunity it presents for practising skills other than one-
to-one casework and its eclectic approach to imparting
skills. It has been widely adopted in day centres, some day
training centres (particularly Sheffield and Pontypridd) and
in many probation offices. Its major use is in the employment field – a Leicestershire scheme, for example, 'was
designed primarily for adult clients of the agency, the only
selection criterion being "clients of the probation service
who are unemployed or threatened with unemploy-
ment" '.[29] Social skills training is one of the new approaches
which has achieved popularity partly as a result of aggres-
sive marketing by a new breed of social work entrepreneurs.

One outcome of the differential treatment approach has
been a focus on *assessment techniques*. The emphasis on
matching client with appropriate treatment calls for improved diagnostic methods. Hand-in-hand with the new
approaches go definite diagnostic criteria.[30] Various
assessment instruments have been used by probation
officers. The Martin Davies index, which seeks to provide
an assessment of risk and need, and the Mooney Problem
Checklist, which involves clients identifying their problems
by ticking boxes on a list, are two favoured approaches.
Most popular though is the Heimler Scale of Social Functioning, which aims to identify areas of satisfaction and

frustration. Another method from the entrepreneurial school of social work innovation, it is actually patented, to be administered only by licensed practitioners – an approach which lends mystique as well as creating a steady market for training courses.

Finally, the developments we have described have led to *organizational change* in the probation service. The general trend has been towards a teamwork approach, envisaged as facilitating the introduction of 'differential treatment' and offering a more comprehensive service to clients. In-service training has encouraged probation officers' inclinations towards teamwork. Participants at a 1977 conference entitled 'Probation: The Team, the Office, the Community', endorsed 'the value of the team approach' and were concerned to: 'provide . . . a greater range of possible opportunities and experiences for clients to draw upon as required'.[31] This approach involves team decisions about allocation, treatment, use of resources and specialization; examples of such developments are documented.[32] Other specializations have followed: court-based teams aim to move back into court and provide an effective social work service in that setting. The Leicestershire Court Intake and Assessment Team adds to this the specialist function of diagnosis by preparing social enquiry reports on all new cases, thus freeing field teams to concentrate on treatment.[33]

MORE OF THE SAME

Having surveyed recent developments, we now examine some of the issues arising. Space dictates that we concentrate on the aspects most pertinent to our analysis and can only note that other problems are posed, such as the relevance of current training and the employment of more unqualified and ancillary staff. We concentrate on the similarities and differences between the new developments and traditional probation work. We start by looking at what is the 'same' and then examine differences which appear to us to consist mainly of 'more of the same'.

'Old Wine in New Bottles'

Elizabeth Wilson applied this biblical reference to the tendency in social work for superficial change to disguise a continuing underlying function.[34] Here we look at ways in which the 'new developments' further the same fundamental aims as traditional tasks and methods. First, these developments continue the theme of *treatment* but in different settings and different ways from one-to-one work. We have already noted the emphasis on 'differential treatment' – the purpose is to increase the effectiveness of treatment by putting together a 'package' to suit each individual client. Day training centres, day centres and hostel provision all share this treatment aim. Stuart Palmer paraphrases the purpose of hostels: 'Residents are sent to the hostel by the courts to be "processed" into honest citizens and then to be "produced" at the other end fully equipped with a job and a place to stay (and if possible a steady girlfriend)'.[35]

Groupwork, even though it moves away from the one-to-one focus, is another form of treatment; in all the examples cited earlier, the group was used as a medium in which to treat individuals. The Central Bristol Area Team Project starts all clients off in a group setting at the beginning of their orders and illustrates this point: 'The induction group focuses on the group member's pattern of law breaking and the circumstances surrounding the offences, leading to the formulation of plans to prevent future law breaking'.[36] This also shows how the orientation of new approaches perpetuates the theme of 'individualization' which we have identified as central to probation work.

Like casework, many of the methods *lack relevance to working-class life.* Family therapy, for example, requires the whole family to meet, focus all their attention on the proceedings and articulate on communication patterns and family functioning. This style of problem solving is no less middle class in orientation than casework and can prove at least equally oppressive. In demanding the regular participation of all family members at set times, it can ignore the irregular routines enforced on families by, for instance, shift-working. Similarly, social skills training seems to aim at imparting middle-class 'life skills' to working-class clients. Elizabeth Burney asks: 'is the articulacy gained more than learning the type of language favoured by probation officers'?[37] It seems arrogant to suppose that our working-class clients necessarily lack the skills to cope with life, or that probation officers appreciate what skills they do need. Do probation officers know at which pubs men are taken on, or how to cope with social interaction on the factory floor? 'Job search' social skills programmes have as one of their aims: 'how to avoid and handle conflict situations at work and so retain your job'.[38] Does that mean the learning of subservience?

Like traditional probation work, many new developments reinforce the *importance of work*. Community service, for instance:

> can provide the offender with a certain amount of control and discipline in terms of behaviour and new relationships which will not be punitive but be of benefit to him in terms of helping him, e.g. an unemployed Community Service offender learns from the work standards required of him by his supervisors and gradually acquires work habits which are sufficient for him to hold down paid employment.[39]

We have shown that employment schemes, hostel regimes and social skills training all pursue this theme and that many day centres specifically aim to return offenders to the labour market. In one of the more extreme examples, the Medway Centre spells this out:

> Factory work . . . involves trainees in the rather monotonous task of assembling plastic plumbing fittings and provides an opportunity to test trainees' reactions in an assembly line situation.

The reality is that many things in life must be accepted at face value. In a real factory situation one may not like the foreman but there is unlikely to be an opportunity to talk this through with him in a group situation. Thus, trainees must come to terms with many aspects of centre life, rather than expect modifications on the part of others.[40]

A final similarity is that the new developments have the same *consensus and integrative assumptions* as traditional probation work. Detached work projects, for instance, operate on unconventional (for the probation service) lines[41] – meeting people on their own ground in pubs or cafés, living in the community and being readily available at home, offering hospitality and a bed for the night – but all this is still with the purpose of making contact with 'those who had been inaccessible and unresponsive to supervision'.[42] The different method is used in an attempt to integrate those most alienated from society. Community service also embodies the idea of integration: 'The provision . . . will enable the offender to give something back to the community against which he has offended'.[43] The underlying assumption is that of a consensus society – those who have broken the rules can be brought back in through social work methods, changed behaviour learnt in a day centre or hostel, or by earning re-acceptance through their own labour in reparation. The idea that the interests of the offender and of society are reconcilable, and indeed identical, is as persistent and pervasive in the new developments as we found it to be in our examination of the major probation tasks.

Although we have argued that our new bottles largely contain old wine, there can be no mistaking the signs that the wine has been fortified. We detect four elements in this strengthening and will look at these in turn.

More Contact

Most of the new developments involve much more extensive contact between probation officers and their clients than traditional approaches. In hostels and day centres, for example, clients and probation officers live, eat and work together to varying degrees. There is huge potential for staff to exercise influence over clients, and more areas of client's lives are exposed to possible scrutiny and control. This can produce problems over a multitude of issues – sexual relationships, drinking, drug use and the irritations of communal living provide just a few examples. Stuart Palmer vividly outlines the conflicts and confusions experienced by staff in a mixed-sex probation hostel when two residents declared their intention to marry and remain at the hostel.[44] Probation staff are anxious about what they might be thought to be condoning and can often find themselves condemning behaviour in clients which they would regard as acceptable in their own lives.

From the clients' point of view, these restrictions are not merely frustrating intrusions on privacy. Behaviour that is unacceptable to staff may be subject to breach action. In his study of breaches, Colin Lawson found that only 3 out of 55 were initiated for 'not being of good behaviour' and all involved conditions of residence in probation hostels. Behaviour in the hostel that did not warrant criminal proceedings caused the wardens to press for breach action.[45] So, behaviour that might ordinarily be ignored, dealt with by admonition or other punishment, if it occurs in a probation hostel could have severe consequences for the residents who find themselves back in court. Despite such problems, accounts of new developments tend to regard extensions of contact as unambiguously in the clients' interests. The Central Bristol Area Team Project describe how they put together packages for individuals, drawing on their various resources and give an example:

Monday:	six hours in the day centre (general support).
Tuesday:	the same, and an evening induction group of one and a half hours.
Wednesday:	the same and one hour one-to-one contact with supervising officer (crisis work).
Thursday:	a.m. two hours' voluntary community

service, p.m. attendance at Thursday Club
7 p.m. to 9 p.m.

Friday: coffee morning a.m. two hours (support
                 and socialization).

Weekend: two hours' contact with volunteer.

This, they proudly point out, represents 29 hours of contact, compared with the national average of half an hour per
week.[46] A formidable package indeed!

More Control

Having noted that increased contact between client and
probation officer may have consequential effects on the
level of control that can be exercised over offenders' behaviour, we can identify other ways in which new
developments shift the role of the probation officer into a
more controlling one. Community service, for example, has
introduced an increased emphasis on regular attendance
and breach action. The NAPO Report on Community Service
comments:

> The nature of the work contains important differences
> from other probation work. It is more directly the imple-
> mentation of a punishment imposed by the court than
> any other probation task and raises, more directly,
> questions of control and authority.
>
> Most areas . . . emphasised that the element of punish-
> ment demanded a firm approach towards those who
> broke their contract with the court. . .[47]

Similarly, in bail hostels probation officers find that their
work may necessitate reporting residents' late arrival back
at night, or other breaches of bail conditions, to the police in
a routine way, a marked shift from their role as 'traditional'
probation officers. There is a growing tendency for participation in new developments to be required as conditions in
probation orders. We have heard of conditions of attend-

ance at a banger-racing scheme, a day centre employment
scheme and an adult literacy project. Such conditions raise
moral, ethical and civil liberties issues, as well as emphasizing the issue of control over the client and increasing the
likelihood of breach actions.

Stronger Messages

In our earlier analysis we noted that an important role of the
probation service was as a bearer of ideology, and that the
main messages of probation work were about the importance of work, leisure and general conformity. The new
developments strengthen these messages in several ways.
First, the increased contact we have already noted exposes
clients more systematically and more often to the 'probation
message'. Second, particular provisions directly emphasize
the value of work and leisure activities. The enormous
expansion of employment schemes of various types under-
lines the 'industriousness' clause in statutory orders and
licences. Activity schemes for young people – adventure
weekends, banger-racing and bike projects go beyond the
traditional encouragement of constructive leisure pursuits
and act as models of appropriate spare-time activity.
Finally, the traditional messages are reinforced by the
recent trend towards the insertion of specific additional
conditions in probation orders. Instead of encouragement
or example, the probation officer can refer to requirements
backed by the authority of the court and by sanctions for
non-compliance.

Alternatives to Imprisonment

Much of this development must be seen against the background of the search for 'alternatives to imprisonment'. To
a large extent the extended contact, increased controls and
stronger messages have been seen as necessary to the provision of tough, realistic and credible alternatives. The
Chief Probation Officer of Inner London spelt it out:

It is important that a day training centre is seen by the public as a viable alternative to imprisonment. The general regime of the centre should appear demanding to those attending, their active participation being expected. Responsibility for the maintenance of discipline within the centre must rest with the Director and staff, and they would have recourse to the courts if necessary through breach proceedings. This would apply in cases of failure to attend or to comply with instructions given by the staff of the centre. . .[48]

There are clear dangers in this argument. At a time when 'law and order' demands are strong it may become increasingly difficult to design 'alternatives' which courts see as 'credible' and use instead of imprisonment. There is already some evidence that new developments, such as community service and probation hostels, are not being used primarily as alternatives to custody.[49] Stricter measures have in any case been introduced in some projects which are not likely to be seen as alternatives.[50] Neither has the introduction of 'alternatives' shown any signs of reducing the prison population, and instead it seems likely that harsher penalties will be used lower down the tariff. Stan Cohen has criticized this 'new network of social control' for reproducing in the community 'the very practices they were designed to replace'. He writes that ' "alternatives" become not alternatives at all, but new programmes which supplement the existing system or else expand the system by attracting new populations – the net of social control is widened'.[51] The new developments in the probation service appear to fall into this trap. Despite their aims – diversification, increased relevance, provision of alternatives to imprisonment – they replicate the characteristics of traditional probation work but in a stricter and more oppressive form.

PART II CRITICAL THEORY

5
The Radical Critique

The late 1960s and early 1970s saw the emergence and development of a radical critique of social work, including the probation service. This fragmented, disparate and limited critique proved an inadequate base for an alternative social work practice but undeniably shook the certainties of social work theory and practice. Here we can only sketch the roots of the critique and will concentrate on the way it has been developed by social workers and, in particular, probation officers. We then consider reactions from different shades of social work opinion and identify its limitations from our own perspective. In this way we locate the issues to tackle in our attempt to construct a more satisfactory theoretical base from which to reach for an alternative probation practice.

THE CRITIQUE OF SOCIAL WORK

For a detailed treatment of the general background, and the different schools of thought which contributed to the emergence of the radical critique, readers are referred to Geoff Pearson's excellent book *The Deviant Imagination*.[1] For our purpose the briefest signposts drawn from his work will suffice. The late 1960s were a time of economic and political upheaval, when the 'post-war consensus' started to dissolve and established attitudes were open to challenge. The radical critique of social work emerged at the same time as 'other professional rumblings'[2] and was heavily influenced by two such developments – the anti-psychiatry movement, based on the works of Laing and Szasz, and advances in sociology, particularly in the sociology of deviance. Anti-psychiatry questioned definitions of madness and inverted accepted 'truths', opening the way for similar questioning of social work assumptions. Deviancy theorists raised doubts about the usefulness of social work intervention because of the implications of labelling theory. By identi-fying social workers as agents of social control, they challenged the traditional assumption that social work is a caring, humane and, above all, essentially helpful process.

These ideas found some support amongst social workers who were disillusioned by their experience of the job. Together with the doubts and conflicts of practice, they were used in developing a critique coming from prac-titioners themselves. This found its most coherent and public articulation through *Case Con*, which described itself as 'A Revolutionary Magazine for Social Workers'. Pro-duced by a collective of social workers from various agencies, it achieved a wide sphere of influence, reflected by the formation around the country of *Case Con* discussion groups. This organizational form facilitated the focus on general social work principles characteristic of *Case Con* but provided no basis for carrying analysis into action. *Case Con* supported action within the relevant trade unions, which tended to erode its own support network and after strug-gling for some time the magazine was wound up in 1977.

The contributions to *Case Con* both recorded the progress made in developing the radical critique and helped to press forward the analysis. The various strands of thought found their way into office discussions and influenced how social workers and probation officers viewed their work. The themes were wide-ranging and targets as varied as the bureaucratic structure of social work agencies and the attempt to professionalize social work. Although the origins of the radical critque lay in liberal, and perhaps anarchic, radicalism, *Case Con* moved towards a marxist perspective as evidenced in its manifesto.[3] The most in-fluential themes were the attack on the casework method and the identification of social work as a part of the state apparatus of social control.

The attack on casework was directed against the variants of psychodynamic casework which dominated theoretical discussion of social work and formed the basis of social work training (though it remains debatable whether it had the same impact on practice). Casework techniques were derived from the world of psychoanalysis and private practice social work in the United States; the orientation was to a highly motivated middle-class clientele and the verbal, reflective, insight-giving approach advocated was seen to be irrelevant and unsuited to the needs, lives and vocabularies of a mainly working-class group of clients. Casework paid no attention to the social and economic position of clients: 'Casework does not have anything to offer towards resolving the national housing shortage, clearing rent arrears, fighting for entitlements from the DHSS, in advocacy at rent tribunals or courts'.[4] Casework was attacked for its ideology of individualization, locating problems in the client rather than the social structure. The key principles said to underpin the method – treating clients as unique individuals, allowing expression of feelings, controlled emotional involvement, acceptance, non-judgemental attitudes, client self-determination and confidentiality – were all found to be compromised in practice.[5] More recently casework has been criticized for its sexist ideology. Elizabeth Wilson argued that Freud's 'paternalistic, authoritarian and contemptuous' attitudes to women had been carried into casework which reinforces traditional family roles and focuses on the mother as client in family situations.[6] Although the critique centred on casework, it also embraced other social work approaches. Examining behaviour therapy, Irwin Epstein concluded that it is as conservative and élitist as casework.[7] At first the radical critique tended uncritically to favour new social work approaches, in particular community and welfare rights work, but later included them as well.[8] The *Case Con* manifesto says:

Social work has expanded to include new (and not so new) tricks, such as community work, group work, wel-

fare rights work etc which when professionalised, end up
by being the same sort of mechanism of control as traditional casework, often with the additional merit of being
less expensive for the ruling class.[9]

At a more general level the critique identified social work
as a part of the state apparatus of social control. Mike
Simpkin, looking back, sums up:

> Criticism of social work centred round the issue of social
> control. Social workers who liked to see themselves as
> being able to help people were in fact merely encouraging
> them to adapt to prevailing conditions, to a sick society
> . . . by focusing on alleged individual inadequacies,
> social workers blinded themselves to the basic material
> needs and encouraged them to tolerate the intolerable.[10]

This strand of the critique suggested that the problems
experienced lay not just in the methods used but in the
structural purpose of social work. This was also identified in
new developments like community work:

> The picture then is one of community workers being
> employed to manipulate and control community pres-
> sure groups' conscious attitude towards the allocation of
> resources, to cool out protest, anger and conflict under
> the guise of 'communication' and 'participation'. When
> the gut issue of lack of resources raises its ugly head the
> community worker has either to keep a 'low profile' or
> placate the angry population by the use of his/her pro-
> fessional skills.[11]

This perspective on social work departed from the consensus view of a benevolent welfare state and was made
possible by, and then encouraged, the development of a
marxist analysis. The *Case Con* manifesto says:

> The welfare state was set up partly in response to
> working class agitation and mainly to stabilise the up-

heavals generated by wartime conditions. It was recognised that improvements in the living conditions of workers helped provide capitalism with a more efficient work force and could nip militancy in the bud. [12]

Relating this to the role of social work Bob Deacon wrote:

> social workers are part of the state apparatus which, in any class society, exists to protect the interests of the ruling class. Social work plays an important ideological role in society by encouraging the belief that complex problems directly caused by capitalism are amenable to social work solutions. [13]

This rudimentary marxist analysis provided a basis for further development.

THE RADICAL CRITIQUE AND PROBATION

In the *Case Con* analysis, comment on the probation service tended to be grafted on as an afterthought. Individual probation officers were involved with *Case Con* and others influenced by its ideas. Generic training encouraged a common cause view and the problems faced by probation officers were seen as 'like those of social workers – only worse'. The early 1970s was a period of considerable agitation in the probation service. Several currents of concern combined in 1972 with the formation of the NAPO Members Action Group (NMAG) as a pressure group within NAPO. Much of NMAGs early activity centred on pay and the democratization of NAPO but it also concerned itself with wider issues affecting the probation service. Its magazine, *Probe*, is more issue-centred and union-focused than *Case Con*. A more compact organizational form has enabled NMAG to continue to exert influence within the service.

An important element in the radical critique of probation work focused on the role of the probation officer. The spur for this development was the pressure exerted by suggested

changes in the work of the service. In particular, the
Younger Report's proposals for a system of 'control in the
community'[14] brought into focus issues of care, control and
coercion, initiating a major debate. Probation officers were
forced to re-examine existing tasks as well as the new proposals and the issues raised were seen as fundamental:

> The Report of the Advisory Council on the Penal System
> confronts each probation officer individually and collect-
> ively in NAPO with a number of issues concerning his job
> and its meaning. The individual must decide what place
> social control has in social work with offenders. NAPO
> must decide whether it is the tool of government or
> whether the probation officer has a role to play in deter-
> mining the nature of his work.[15]

The focus of the ensuing debate was not on the general
issue of social work as a form of social control but specifically upon the role of controls within probation work. The
radical response rejected the proposed increase in the
controlling functions of probation officers. The struggle to
prevent change affected the way the debate was conducted
and the radical argument was less fundamental than that
advanced in *Case Con*. The issue polarized into 'care versus
control', with radicals emphasizing that social work help
was the most effective approach:

> But there is now a drift away from the use of controls in
> exercising supervision. They have been found to be more
> effective in theory than in practice and they have been
> counter-productive leading to an impairment of the pro-
> bation officer's ability to offer the social work help his
> training equips him to offer.[16]

Although this approach tended towards uncritical acclaim
of social work, the discussions succeeded in highlighting
the tensions inherent in the probation officer's role:

> Many of the difficulties which exist in the role of the

probation officer arise because there are dual demands
placed on him and that these demands can often be in
conflict and provide a source of tension. On the one hand
the probation officer is expected to uphold the law and
seek to correct offenders who have broken the law. This
is an expectation that he will be an agent of social control.
On the other hand he is expected to advise, assist and
befriend the offender, to offer him help and have his
interests at heart. [17]

Within the radical response there was some recognition that
the care/control split was an oversimplification:

all attempts by the State to help an individual are less
than altruistic and contain some element of the exercise
of social control over his individuality. Probation officers
have tended to gloss over the conflict between social
control and helping activity. [18]

But this remained a muted theme. The pressure for change
was identified as the continuation of a drift already under
way. The probation service had accepted parole in 1967 and
community service in 1972 (not without some opposition)
and these measures were seen as having introduced the
control elements Younger sought to expand. The phrase
'screws on wheels' was coined and widely used as a description which dramatized the role probation officers
would be playing if this trend continued. The 'care versus
control' debate continues to reverberate within the service.

In 1976, NMAG produced a working document which
took the radical critique much further and, like the *Case Con*
manifesto, set out on a specifically marxist analysis. It was
produced collectively as an attempt to crystallize and advance the group's thinking. The critique of probation work
set out in the working document shares the elements identified in the radical critique of social work. Sections deal with
the management and structure of the service, the role of
training and the issue of professionalism, as well as the

central concern of probation practice. It echoes the themes
of the attack on casework:

> the probation service makes little effort to exert pressure
> for social change. On the contrary, the overwhelming
> emphasis is on effecting changes in the personality and
> attitudes of the offender with little regard to the nature of
> the social circumstances to which he is expected to adapt.

and on individualization says:

> The social worker or probation officer intervenes on a
> personalised basis. The probation officer is not to con-
> centrate on why there is, for instance, so much
> unemployment or homelessness but instead to focus on
> why a particular client cannot hold down a job or keep
> accommodation.[19]

The probation service is firmly located as an agency of
social control within the state apparatus:

> The probation service's concentration on personal
> change is a consequence of its structural position in
> society. It is a small part of society's system of 'law and
> order'. Together with the more central social control
> mechanisms such as the army, the police and the judi-
> ciary, the probation service plays its part in preserving
> social definitions and ensuring the stability of the present
> regime. With the development of the Welfare State ethic,
> social control mechanisms have become more subtle and
> covert than in previous eras and this has produced a
> useful role for the probation service (and other social
> work agencies).[20]

Although care and control is still identified as a significant
duality the working document does not dwell on the issue
of specific controls in probation but rather concentrates on
the general social control functions of its social work orientation. The individualization of deviance, the 'cooling out'

of both client anger and wider concern about social problems, 'special pleading' to cover up defects in welfare provision, helping to maintain the workforce, acting as a 'sop to the liberal conscience', adopting a correctional approach to deviance, distracting from real social problems and legitimating the present social system were all identified as significant elements.

In probation, as well as general issues such as housing and income maintenance, the radical critique is also necessarily concerned with wider issues concerning the criminal justice system. Criticism of prison regimes or sentencing practice is not restricted to radicals but is shared by many probation officers. In this area NMAG members were influenced by formal and informal contacts with groups like RAP, PROP, NCCL, National Deviancy Conference and LAG. NMAG advanced its position from a general one of campaigning for penal reform (Statement of Aims 1972) to a more specific one including an abolitionist stance on imprisonment, decrminalization of a wide range of offences, opposing the shift to a more correctional service and seeking to minimize the repressive elements of the work (Statement of Aims 1976). Inevitably the development of this strand of the radical critique was piecemeal rather than comprehensive and drew upon disparate sources. The influence of RAP and of Thomas Mathieson[21] contributed to the adoption of an abolitionist position. The policy of decriminalization emerged in response to a Home Office review of the vagrancy acts.[22] Philip Bean's attack on rehabilitation[23] had some impact and contributed to the adoption of policies such as withdrawal from prison welfare and abolition of parole. These examples illustrate the hybrid nature of the radical critique of the criminal justice system.

We have traced the development of the major strands of the radical critique of probation and social work, ending our account with the state of thinking in the mid-1970s – an arbitrary point to stop but corresponding roughly to the emergence of the 'early critique'. We have noted its considerable impact: some parts have commanded widespread acceptance while other, more fundamental, aspects have

proved harder to swallow. The world of social work certainties has been shaken and we turn now to look at some
reactions from within social work, concentrating on probation.

REACTIONS TO THE RADICAL CRITIQUE

From the first the radical critique has come under fire from
several quarters. Here we look at these reactions under four
general heads – hostile opposition from conservative elements, the mainstream reaction of incorporating some
peripheral facets of the critique, the newly emerging elaborated response from some social work thinkers and, finally,
the development of the critique through application of a
fuller and more sophisticated marxist analysis.

Conservative Hostility

The radical critique has attracted criticism from the extreme
right. *The Gould Report*, which examined the effect of
marxist and radical ideas in higher education, singles out
social work, and NMAG in particular, for attack. The report
(which has been likened to a McCarthyist witch-hunt)[24]
claimed that 'many generic social work courses consist of
little more than systematic indoctrination of students in
sectarian political ideas'.[25]

In the same vein Ron Lewis, a senior probation officer, in
his contribution to *The Black Papers on Education* wrote:

By far the most sinister manifestations of academic interference with social work comes from the body calling
itself the National Deviancy Conference. . . . It operates
by holding symposia, the chief message of which seems
to be that good is bad . . . and that bad is good. . . . They
also liaise with many of the fringe revolutionary groups,
which having recruited few law abiding people, now
pursue the law breakers. Such groups organise rent
strikes, squatting and give support to, if not actually

organise, prison riots. . . .They are advocating or giving
support to, lawlessness, including acts of violence.

He added:

The Probation Officers Action Group . . . is a striking
example of the success which these radical academics
have achieved.[26]

These extracts illustrate how the extreme right grotesquely
distorts the position of those with whom they disagree,
seeking to discredit and eliminate alternative ideas from
social work education and thinking. They also oversimplify
the developments on which they comment and over-
estimate the links between radical academics and practitioners.

NMAG faced hostile opposition from the leadership of
NAPO and some of the most severe attacks on radical
probation officers have been launched from within the
union. This reached its peak in 1977, when Donald Bell, then
general secretary of NAPO, attacked the working document,
claiming that support for it could not be reconciled with
membership of NAPO. He wrote: 'The members of the
Association therefore have a clear choice to make. Should
they take steps of some kind to ensure that all members
uphold the objects to which they have subscribed. . .?'[27]

It was not long before this invitation was taken up by
Murray Bruggen (then chairman), who took it upon himself
to rule that some issues could not even be debated within
NAPO. At the 1977 AGM Lord Hunt (then president) made it
clear in his address that those who agreed with the working
document ought to consider whether they should remain in
the probation service. This red scare in miniature reached
its climax in 1978 when the London branch of NAPO was
suspended from the union for its continued participation in
picketing at Grunwick, an activity ruled inconsistent with
NAPO's objects. Membership rejected this course of confrontation and reinstated the branch. The attack on the

radical viewpoint, and the radicals themselves, has receded for the moment.

Management within the probation service has also criticized those with radical views, often by implying that they are immature, unstable or unable to cope with authority. One chief probation officer addressing his staff explained:

> Since no human society is ideal, for some it may be easier to turn from their client's shortcomings and their own imperfections to the imperfections of society. If only there could be one mighty overthrow of the system then social justice would be achieved and all would be sweetness and light: this is a stereotype of adolescent thinking, and we all have an adolescent inside us trying to get out.[28]

Although others have blamed social work educators for encouraging radicalism, criticism has also come from those involved in social work education. Robert Pinker wrote:

> In my opinion the politicisation of any professional activity is an abuse of trust. . . . Perhaps our earlier generations of social workers were wise enough to know that their occupational credibility rested exclusively on their professional knowledge, and their special capacity to provide the sort of help their clients needed. They did not blur the lines between their professional responsibility and the general field of political activity. . . . Whether or not all life's tragedies can be attributed to social or economic injustice, the redress of these injustices is no more the primary task of social workers than it is of doctors, nurses, teachers or lawyers.[29]

A social work teacher much admired by the conservative school, Brian Munday, believes that radical ideas are so alarming that their impact on social work courses should be contained by the careful selection of students – admitting those mature enough to cope, and by restricting course content so that 'not too much negative material is concentrated at any one time'.[30] *The Gould Report*'s characterization of social work courses as 'radical indoctrination' is manifestly absurd – the impact of radical ideas on social work courses is both patchy and limited, with most courses remaining steadfastly conservative.

Finally the radical critique has been criticized by practising social workers and probation officers. As well as themes already covered, a common form is that recorded by Stan Cohen: 'however interesting, amusing, correct and even morally uplifting our message might be, it is ultimately a luxury which cannot be afforded by anyone tied down by the day-to-day demands of a social work job'.[31] The critique is said to be too abstract, having little connection with the immediate problems of practice. Radicals are challenged to show how their work differs or to produce a blue-print for a social work practice consistent with their critique.

Mainstream Incorporation

The radical critique has influenced mainstream social work, and there have been many attempts to adjust to its impact. In the main these have consisted of an incorporation of the vocabulary or of some of the peripheral themes of the critique rather than any fundamental restructuring of social work theory or practice. While some social work agencies remain hostile, others have welcomed and encouraged 'bright, young radicals' because they lend an appearance of progressiveness. Thus advertisements may stress new developments in an area. In the probation service day centres, intake teams and even court-based teams are presented with a radical flourish. Gary Clapton pinpoints the superficial nature of this radicalism: 'the cult of radicalism appears to have become a commodity within the social services industry itself . . . the movement has been appropriated as a means of improving and refreshing the social services, instead of questioning their existence and function'.[32]

Many training courses have changed to accommodate some of the new ideas and concepts, often in response to

demands from students. Geoff Mungham says: 'The direction of instruction and pedagogy is slowly away from more
traditional therapeutic concerns, towards the rather more
impersonal socio-structural orientations', but warns that
pressure from students can be 'co-opted and comfortably
accommodated within pre-existing professional, organisa-
tional and ideological structures'.[33]

Some social work methods are presented as providing
some answers to the radical critique: for example group
work because it does not individualize clients totally and
community work because of its broader base. The latest
innovation in social work theory, systems theory or the
integrated method, has been presented as a means of reconciling traditional social work and the radical critique on the
basis that it talks of both environmental and individual
change. Commenting on the Pincus and Minahan version,
Armstrong and Gill comment:

> Their application of systems theory provides more gloss
> than substance. All they offer is a description of the
> inter-relationships between various social work systems.
> Such a description does not take us very far forward. . . .
> This unquestioning view of social systems is one of the
> ideological assumptions which prevent the unitary
> approach from adequately incorporating conflict, there-
> by limiting its relevance for the analysis of social
> problems.[34]

Despite its novel progressive-sounding jargon the integrated approach is noticeably weak on the methods to be
used to produce change in environmental systems. The
latest contender for the 'radical social work' title cannot
satisfy the radical critique.

A similar picture is found in social work practice. The
environment is now accepted as a target for social work
intervention; BASW have incorporated in their definition of
social work 'agent of social change' as a legitimate role
'using knowledge obtained from practice to attempt to

modify the social environment to make it more conducive to social well-being'.[35]

We have shown in our earlier analysis of probation tasks how probation officers have tried to respond to issues raised by the radical critique, for instance by consciously including comment on socio-economic and environmental factors in their social enquiry reports but that such excursions are both cautious and peripheral to their work. Rather crude conceptions of labelling theory have similarly been instrumental in engendering support for the juvenile bureau schemes set up under the 1969 Children and Young Persons Act and in creating enthusiasm in the probation service for Schur's 'radical non-intervention' strategy.[36]

A recent example of incorporation in the probation field is the attempt by Tony Bottoms and Bill McWilliams to construct a 'paradigm for practice' starting from the radical critique's view that 'the treatment model is theoretically faulty and capable of injustice'.[37] They propose a tinkering with the mechanics of probation, based on a split between care and control functions, arguing that probation supervision should be unambiguously regarded as surveillance with the frequency of reporting laid down by the court and enforced consistently by the probation officer. Within that framework 'treatment' is to be replaced by 'unconditional help', though they substantially qualify the boundaries of 'unconditional help'. The probationer is to be free to accept or reject help without adverse consequences. They also propose changes in social enquiry report practice and recommend that the probation service develops micro-structural community intervention as a crime prevention strategy. Some elements of this 'paradigm' will be superficially attractive to probation officers influenced by the radical perspective but the model is extremely weak in parts (the crime prevention strategy being the outstanding example) and is unsoundly grounded. The proposal illustrates the dangers of a partial approach to the radical analysis. Because Bottoms and McWilliams fail to confront fully the reasons for the failure of treatment and work in a political vacuum, they propose a practice which could be more oppressive for probation officers and more repressive for clients.

Elaborated Social Work Responses

Paul Halmos has given attention to the radical critique's connection of politics and social work. He says his recent book is 'about the predicament of those who, in trying to better the condition of man, are caught between deep and private needs on the one hand and grave public demands on the other'. Yet he does his best to discredit the left position: 'Not unlike adolescents having a smoke in the school lavatory, Marxists furtively contemplate the spiritual consolations and fascinations of the great dialectical balance'.[38]

His response to the conflict he identifies between the personal and the political lies in 'equilibration' but that is to be maintained by keeping the two separate: 'The division of labour in society has proved to be a good thing for men, and it is not immediately obvious why personal and political activism should not be kept separate'.[39]

So, although equilibrium suggests a balance, it is clear that Halmos means that politics should be kept out of social work:

It is fundamental to my position that a man can play the role of father of his son, and son of his father, but he can never play the two roles at the same time, he can never conflate, merge or hybridise the two roles. Analogously there is no hybrid professional role of social worker cum political activist. A social worker can take time off to act politically as an informed and professionally trained citizen. Similarly, a political change agent can and does act as a private citizen from time to time, whatever his political identity. If either attempts to be both at the same time there will be difficulties; the zebra-like composite creature will wonder whether he is a black-striped white animal or a white-striped black one.[40]

This passage, apart from combining an awful analogy with

a muddled metaphor, confirms that this elaborated response is only an extended version of the conservative response described earlier.

A writer who commands some respect from radicals, notably through his work with and writing on claimants' unions, is Bill Jordan.[41] He is identified with some aspects of the radical analysis and criticizes how social work has curtailed the freedom and citizenship of its clients;[42] he has attacked both casework and behaviour therapy for their middle-class orientation and seems to understand the practice predicaments facing social workers and probation officers.[43] His criticism extends to the social security system and fundamental to his solution is a 'Welfare State which balances the concepts of citizenship, personal liberty and state intervention'.[44] He is not clear on how that is to be achieved but regards good social work as a key contribution. His prescriptions are attractive but deal almost exclusively with personal attributes and approaches. Thus social workers and probation officers should deal with clients in an open and honest way so that they can strive together towards an ideal of fellow citizenship; they should fight alongside, empathize with them, use their own personality, be flexible, sensitive and self-critical.

In his most recent work, Bill Jordan fills pages with examples of his own practice as if to say, learn from my mistakes, practise like me and you will overcome! The right sort of practice can help bring about social reform:

> changes in social policy and administration have made social work a more political activity, and have given social workers more political sophistication. But ultimately the confidence to argue for a constructive programme for change must rest on the good quality of its work in professional tasks. As social workers begin to rediscover their faith in themselves as helpers they may also once again find their courage and their voices. Instead of using much of their energy resisting their organisation they may find ways of uniting with their managers to demand a better life for their clients.[45]

The evangelistic tone of Bill Jordan's work reflects the personalized nature of the solutions he proffers. Although incorporating parts of the radical critique in his analysis, he largely ignores structural and political problems in his prescriptions. The individual social worker is left to shoulder the burden of guilt for inadequate practice when problems are not resolved.

A similar line can be identified in a recent article by Bruce Hugman in which, starting from a position 'much persuaded by the insights of marxist analysis but nevertheless committed to democratic solutions',[46] he seeks to identify radical and socialist practices for probation officers. Although based on the radical critique, reflecting a clear understanding of the problems and placing some emphasis on collective solutions, the article consistently underestimates structural and political problems, arguing for instance that 'we must ensure that we are represented in places where major decisions are made (on Probation Committees, for example). . . . Determined and skilful groups of people with original and coherent proposals can and do bring about change'.[47] At the level of methods he uncritically supports approaches such as day training centres, group work and community involvement, which raise the same issues as traditional practice, and advocates the Bottoms and McWilliams 'paradigm', which might be more repressive. Like Bill Jordan, his underlying emphasis is on the ability of the individual probation officer to transcend the problems encountered:

> The effective radical socialist will have at his command a whole range of tactics and styles; he will use serious rational argument as well as humour; he will search out common interests as a basis for collective action and he will also canvass and persuade individuals; he will not become enmeshed in jargon and procedures; he will not be boring; he will interest and intrigue people . . .; he will be skilful, subtle, persistent, adaptable; he will not see compromise only as betrayal, but as sometimes a means to real change; he will keep his options open to avoid

both the dismissive label 'extremist' and the dangers of absorption.[48]

A tall order for the aspiring radical!

Marxist Developments

The early radical critique, as represented by both *Case Con* and NMAG, moved towards a marxist analysis. This development parallelled the rediscovery of marxist thought in the related disciplines of economics, social history, sociology – including criminology – and social policy. This creative burgeoning of marxist analysis has continued and accelerated since the mid-1970s. Major works on social policy by Cynthia Cockburn,[49] Elizabeth Wilson,[50] Ian Gough[51] and Norman Ginsburg[52] have all touched on social work and related issues. Chris Jones has produced important material on the history of social work.[53] Peter Leonard and Paul Corrigan addressed themselves specifically to the development of a marxist approach to social work.[54] Of relevance to probation work have been major works in criminology, for example *Policing the Crisis* by Stuart Hall *et al.*[55] and published collections of papers from the National Deviancy Conference.[56]

This rapid development of theory has tended to leave the practitioners behind. *Case Con* has folded and there seems to be no equivalent organization of social workers growing in its place. NMAG has survived and maintained its development. The original marxist analysis advanced in the working document has been superseded although there has been no coherent replacement as a statement of NMAG's position. In the next two chapters we attempt to relate some of the newer theoretical developments to the field of probation practice. The first step must be to identify what we now regard as limitations in the early radical critique of probation work.

LIMITATIONS OF THE RADICAL CRITIQUE

The marxist analysis presented in NMAG's working document now requires considerable modification, development and refinement. For instance, it was over-deterministic and underplayed the importance of ideology. Both the state and the role of law were presented as directly expressive of ruling-class interests. The analysis of the welfare state and its significance was similarly oversimplified.

These basic theoretical inadequacies meant that the position of the probation service in the state apparatus could not be clearly understood. Tentatively the probation service was identified as a part of the welfare state but more firmly seen as part of the state's 'law and order' function. The significance of these locations was only sketchily suggested; the relative contribution of the probation service was unclear; and the ways in which its structural role was carried out were not developed.

These factors contributed to a third problem of the critique – an over-simplification and separation of the notions of care and control. Part of the search for radical practice became 'the attempt to extricate the "caring" elements of social work practice and ideology from the dehumanising and controlling elements of bureaucratic control'.[57] Insufficient attention was therefore given to an analysis of social work help, hindering the development of a more rigorous critique of probation work.

The analysis was also too generalized and insufficiently related to specific probation tasks. This lack of detailed connection had two adverse effects. First, it created a sense of distance between the critique and day-to-day work so that some were unable to accept the arguments made. Second, those who did accept the critique were unable to use it directly in evaluating particular tasks.

Probation officers were often confused about how to carry the critique into their everyday work. Its over-deterministic tendency led to what Norman Ginsburg described as: 'the rejection of social work as a form of complete social control and class collaboration'.[58] A more common reaction was to join the hunt for a 'radical social work' with more emphasis on method and novelty than purpose and effect.

Because of the problems we have outlined, the radical critique offered practitioners insufficient guidance in arriving at a practice consistent with analysis and progressive in effect. The search for 'radical social work' has led people up some unlikely blind alleys. Anything new and different is seen as potentially radical and with no criteria for evaluation can hardly be opposed. The danger is, as John Clarke pointed out: 'the reference point used to assess whether or not some aspect of practice is radical tends to become the existing structure of the agency itself'.[59]

Another tendency is to judge radicalism by the position of management. The touchstone of radicalism then becomes any anti-management stance, any action of which the hierarchy disapproves or anything which is outspoken or slightly shocking. These criteria are a poor alternative for the clear analysis and programme for practice which is needed.

Finally the radical critique lacked coherence. Because the marxist analysis was unrefined and incomplete, other sometimes inconsistent lines of thought were grafted on. The different strands of the critique could not be united and important issues could not be explored adequately. Terms such as 'agent of social control' were used freely but not precisely, so that an appreciation of how and why social control is exercised could not be developed. This lack of coherence hampered the development of a fuller marxist analysis of the role of the probation officer.

In the next chapter we present a marxist analysis which we hope overcomes the shortcomings of the early radical critique and in the chapter following that we relate that theory specifically to the work of the probation service.

6
Towards a Marxist Critique

The radical critique, in seeking to understand the problems encountered in social work and probation practice, quickly moved towards explanations based on a marxist analysis. Our experience leads us to believe that other explanations are unsatisfactorily superficial and inadequate. Only a marxist perspective can illuminate the connections between our work and crucial economic, structural and political issues. Recent marxist theory has focused on a theory of the state which we have found particularly useful. This theory places the development of the state and its institutions in a historical perspective, showing how different parts of society are related and the significance of those relationships. It provides a way of looking at the state and its institutions showing how apparently contradictory and illogical developments have an underlying coherence. In this chapter we set out a theory of the state, paying particular attention to the welfare state and the criminal justice system.

THE STATE

The writings of Marx and Engels do not provide an elaborated theory of the state but others have developed relevant elements of their work.[1] A recent upsurge of interest in this theory means that a lively debate continues and no single 'correct' account can be identified. New theorists have applied these ideas to a whole range of disciplines, including those related to probation work, and we shall be drawing out from their work those parts we have found most relevant and useful. Our aim is to present these concepts simply and clearly for those whose familiarity with such theory is limited. Throughout the text we acknowledge our sources and readers are advised to turn to them for further reading and a fuller examination of the issues presented.

Capitalism

The essence of the marxist approach is that society and the state can only be understood in relation to the economic system – the way in which wealth is produced. We live in a capitalist economy, which although modified somewhat by state intervention, remains fundamentally capitalist. Such an economic system is one in which the means of production – the means by which wealth is produced – is in the hands of a small group, the holders of capital, who are the ruling class. The means of production cannot alone create wealth and the labour power of working people must be employed to realize that goal. But the working class receives back in the form of wages only a part of the wealth it produces. The rest, in marxist terms surplus value, is kept by the ruling-class owners of capital in the form of profit so that they accumulate more capital. Right at the heart of the capitalist system lies this unequal relationship between those who own the means of production – the capitalist class – and those from whom surplus value is extracted – the working class. The labour power of the worker is sold to the capitalist on the basis of apparent equality. This appearance is deceptive because unless workers are prepared to enter this unequal relationship they have no means of survivival. The formal equality of the relationship disguises its true nature, that of exploitation. This outline is over-simplified and skeletal but provides a sufficient base for our argument.[2]

Class Divisions

An inevitable consequence of this system of producing wealth is that there are two main classes in society potentially always in conflict – the ruling-class owners of capital, and the working-class sellers of labour. A fundamental contradiction of the system is that, although working-class labour is crucial to the continuation of capitalism, this organized labour force continually creates problems for capitalism as it seeks to improve wages and conditions, thus claiming a larger share of surplus value. There is then always potential antagonism between these two classes.

Having noted this main class division, it is immediately obvious that not all the population can be slotted into one or other of these groups. Like many others, probation officers seem to fit into neither class. There has been considerable discussion of the class position of such workers. Probation officers have no access to the means of production and sell their labour for a wage. On the other hand they do not directly produce surplus value. However, we will argue that, by encouraging the values and attitudes underpinning capitalism, probation officers perform an important ideological role for that system.

The class nature of our society is revealed in many ways. Probation officers deal mostly with working-class clients and every day encounter evidence of enormous inequality in terms of income, housing, education and living standards between them and the wealthy ruling class. The Royal Commission on the Distribution of Income and Wealth showed that in 1976 the wealthiest 10 per cent of the population owned 60.6 per cent of total personal wealth and this has been criticized as an underestimate.[3] Despite such clear class divisions, issues in society are never discussed in these terms and the enormous gap between rich and poor is rarely explicitly raised. Instead, appeals are made to 'the British people' or to 'the national interest', as if all are equal. The divisions used in discussing society are rarely those of class – people are grouped in other ways, for example as patients, tenants, ratepayers, consumers or clients. While these categories convey some shared interests, they ignore the issue of class and divert attention from the fundamental division in society.[4]

The State – Representing Whose Interests?

In *The Manifesto of the Communist Party* Marx and Engels claim that the executive of the modern state is a committee for managing the common affairs of capitalists.[5] Although that is clearly an over-statement, it is obvious that there are strong connections between the owners of capital and the governing institutions of the state. Three main connections are:

(1) The people who head the state. Ralph Miliband writes:

> the people who are located in the commanding heights of the state, in the executive, administrative, judicial, repressive and legislative branches, have tended to belong to the same class or classes which have dominated the other strategic heights of the society, notably the economic and cultural ones.[6]

Examples of this abound:

> Barings is the oldest of the merchant banks and there are five separate Baring peerages; Cromer, Northbrook, Revelstoke, Ashburton and Howick. They have provided two Chancellors of the Exchequer, a Governor of India, a Lord Chamberlain, a Governor of Kenya and a former Governor of the Bank of England – Lord Cromer.[7]

Interestingly, Mrs Susan Baring is an influential member of the Central Council of Probation and After-Care Committees and of the Employers' Side of the Probation Service Joint Negotiating Committee.

(2) The capitalist class can wield power over the state because of its ownership and control of economic resources. Pressure is exerted in many ways, for example through the formal channel of the Confederation of British Industry, indirectly through the newspapers they own or individually through investment decisions.

(3) The state is subject to constraints because it operates in the context of an international capitalist economic system

and so must bow to the global requirements of capital. This helps us understand the significance of the directive given by the International Monetary Fund to the Labour government in 1974. In an attempt to bolster a failing economy. Healey accepted the conditions set by international capitalism and the burden was placed on working people. Health and education services were cut; gas, electricity and transport prices rose; pay restraint was imposed and the weight of taxation was further transferred on to working people – all this to create a shift of wealth into company profits.[8]

These connections and powerful modes of pressure ensure that the state is strongly influenced by the interests of capital.[9]

The State – A Degree of Independence

In arguing that the state is a capitalist state we do not mean that it is always and directly expressive of the needs of capital. The state has a degree of independence. One reason that this is so is because capital itself needs the state to act as an 'ideal total capitalist', reconciling competing interests within the capitalist class. The other reason is that the state is the result of years of class struggle. The working class has fought back to improve its lot and one result of this is that some state activities are concessions which represent a cost to capital. Some examples of state activity which benefit the working class are the National Health Service, education, unemployment benefits, old age pensions and council housing.

State functions which represent a gain for the working class are extremely contradictory because they also provide benefits for capitalism. For example, the National Health Service has obviously helped to improve the health and general condition of working people. But it also benefits the owners of capital to have a healthy, strong labour force who will not be off sick or operating under par. In this respect the state carries out tasks for capitalism as a whole, relieving individual employers from attending to these needs of their workers. Under capitalism, state activities cannot be understood in a simple and straightforward way: reforms often have contradictory consequences, a fact which socialist programmes based on expanded state provisions frequently neglect.

To summarize, we can say that although the state is concerned with the interests of the ruling class as a whole, there is a degree of separation from their direct concerns, sometimes called 'relative autonomy'. The state will tend to respond to the long-term needs of capital but is also shaped by the outcome of working-class struggles and capitalist concessions.[10]

The State Form

The state is usually thought of as a set of institutions – hospitals, schools, prisons, probation offices, etc., but it should also be understood as a set of social relations. Just as capitalism does not simply mean a collection of factories and financial institutions but also the unequal relationship between capital and labour, so the state connotes a set of relations which can be called the state form. These relations include, for example, the hierarchical and bureaucratic way in which state institutions are structured. This helps to explain the way in which even services representing a gain for the working class, such as social security and council housing, are delivered in a way often experienced by recipients as alien, intrusive and unhelpful. The state form is pervasive and enduring so that proposals such as a single salary scale or seniorless teams within the probation service have met fierce resistance because they represent a challenge to social relations functional to capitalism.[11]

Surface Appearance and Real Relations

We have explained what we understand to be the connections between the state and the ruling class. However, these connections are rarely seen and the state is more often perceived as a 'thing apart', acting over and above class interest, as the reconciler of those interests. The 'relative autonomy' of the state cannot alone account for this false appearance. To help us understand this effect it is useful to consider the marxist concept of 'fetishized form'. This means that what is observed is a surface effect concealing underlying fundamental relationships.

Marx instances the central example of wage labour as an illustration of the fetishized form. Under capitalism labourers go to the factory, sell their labour and in return receive wages. This relationship is perceived as a contract – 'a fair day's wage for a fair day's work' – and disputes are usually framed in these terms. But the surface appearance of the wage contract hides the exploitative nature of the fundamental relationship between capital and labour – the extraction of surplus value.

A parallel effect influences perceptions of the state. Capitalist class interest, which forms the basis for much state activity, is concealed by the surface appearance of 'the neutral state'. The state is a fetishized form and its neutral appearance is preserved through various forms of impersonal authority:

> the rule of law, the bureaucratic process and parliaments which have the authority of 'the people'. Liberal democracy transforms people into a mass of subjects with certain legal rights. These rights fail to recognise, indeed necessarily deny real inequalities between individuals. Class divisions disappear in the face of this abstract individualism.[12]

In the Service of Capital

The state organizes social and political life so as to make possible the accumulation of capital through the continued expansion of production. Two major tasks are the reproduction of labour – ensuring that there is always a labour force, fit, healthy and available to produce surplus value – and the reproduction of capitalist social relations – ensuring that the working class has the education, skills, training, discipline, motivation and attitudes necessary in the work-force.

The state acts as an organizer to make society a profitable site for capitalist investments in three distinct ways. In the *economic sphere* it has assumed an increasingly important role as capitalism has moved into a state monopoly form. Examples of this organizing role are the repeated use of wage restraint to increase profits and the massive grants given to industry as financial inducements to investment. Second, the state organizes in the *ideological sphere* to promote a set of beliefs and values which support the status quo. This is done through the state education system but reinforced through public information announcements and campaigns, through the media and the orchestration of public opinion. Indirectly the state form educates people about their role and position in society – for example the Inland Revenue and DHSS convey the subordinate position of women, and our political system 'educates' people to think that a vote cast every few years is the only necessary political activity. Third, the state organizes in the *legal-juridical sphere*, through the civil and criminal law. Here the rules that govern behaviour are set and enforced. We return to examine this aspect in greater detail later in this chapter. [13]

Coercion and Consent

In its ideological work the state seeks to achieve the same kind of authority throughout society that capital exercises in the economic sphere. Such ideological dominance is known in marxist theory as 'hegemony' and is achieved when: 'a particular ruling class alliance has managed to secure through the state such a total social authority, such decisive cultural and ideological leadership, over the subordinate classes that it shapes the whole direction of social life in its image'. [14] When this happens there appears to exist in society a consensus; consent is given by the population to the general direction imposed on social life by the dominant group. This domination appears to be universal – what everyone wants, as well as legitimate – not won through coercive measures.

Generally the state works through a combination of two measures: coercion and consent. When hegemony is achieved consent is the key, legitimating support but is always backed by the state's reserve power of coercion. If consent is withdrawn by significant sections of the population the balance between consent and coercion alters. At such times of 'crisis in hegemony' or breakdown of consensus, coercive measures become more prominent. In this tilt towards coercion, state intervention becomes more overt. The state seeks to organize consent for the legitimated used of the reserves of force upon which it ultimately rests. This may be a risky venture for the state, since the use of force may produce a backlash leading to further withdrawal of consent.

Those who have interpreted recent British history[15] along these lines suggest that a period of successful hegemony was managed in the 1950s, made possible by an economic upswing which allowed surplus value to be channelled into the welfare activities of the state. Since then, closely linked to crises in the economic sphere, successive crises in hegemony have occurred and the consensus has assumed a rather fragile appearance. The withdrawal of consent has been signalled by the re-emergence of militant trade unionism, the formation of self-help groupings like tenants' associations, claimants' unions, squatters' organizations, PROP, etc., and the development of the anti-war movement and student unrest in the late 1960s. In response to this crisis, there has been a shift to more coercive measures and gradually the more repressive features of the state have been used to deal with dissent in its various forms.[16] Even during this coercive tilt the consent of the majority is secured for strong action. This is managed by several means: the construction of moral panics around issues like 'mugging' and terrorism; the desensitization of the public to previously controversial issues such as arming the police and using the army in aid of the civil power; the defining out of opposition as the work of 'mindless militants' and 'extremist infiltration'; and by appeal to the real fears of working people about change and loss of security. We think this development is significant for the probation service and return to discuss its implications in the next chapter.[17]

THE WELFARE STATE

There are no clear boundaries to the welfare state but the term is generally taken to mean those parts of the state's activity connected with the population's well-being: council housing, the National Health Service, social security and social services, for example. These activities have expanded over the last 70 years and are often counterposed to other state functions such as economic intervention or defence. Welfare state functions are often portrayed as the 'good' part of the state, compared to the 'bad', repressive aspects such as the police, army and prisons. The idea that we already live in a 'welfare state' and the promise of Fabian socialism that increased state intervention will bring about a socialist society both create considerable confusion. Our analysis suggests that such simplifications are misleading because all state activity also serves capitalism.

As understanding of the particular significance of welfare provision is important for probation officers. This provides the background against which the role of social work generally must be considered. In their work, probation officers deal daily with the welfare state agencies over housing problems, liaison with schools, cooperation with doctors and negotiation with the DHSS.

The Growth of Welfare

Common views are that welfare state provision is a sign of general progress in society or that such provision has resulted from the struggles of the working class and so serves its interests. Direct experience teaches us that although services available in the welfare state are potentially useful to working people this is not how people find them to be in practice. They are not only inadequate but often inaccessible and usually delivered in an unhelpful way. Working people certainly do not consider that state services belong to them and commonly regard them with suspicion. If we look more closely at how the welfare state developed we can understand this better. It becomes apparent that it did not develop in a simple linear, cause–effect–beneficial consequence way but rather grew out of a complex of interacting influences, conflicts, events and decisions which had contradictory consequences. Here we identify three strands in the development of the welfare state.

Direct Working-Class Action

There are few examples of working-class action based on direct welfare demands. Paul Corrigan quotes one instance during World War I when Clydeside munitions workers threatened a general strike if the government did not intervene to prevent rent rises. Within a few days the government had banned all rent increases.[18] However, such direct working-class welfare demands have played a minor role in the creation of the welfare state.

General Working-Class Pressure

More significant in the development of welfare policies has been the direct and indirect pressure of the working class and ruling class fear of outright class conflict. This is sometimes openly acknowledged as in Balfour's assertion that social reform is the 'most effective antidote' to socialism.[19] The growth of welfare is a complex process. Sometimes direct pressure from the working class (often on non-welfare demands) is defused, partly by concessions in the field of welfare. Sometimes reforms seek to pre-empt pressure from the working class, and prevent the spread of agitation by easing conditions – the effect of indirect pressure. In this process real benefits are won but rarely in the form that the working class has sought.

The huge expansion of welfare provision following World War II was part of 'the post-war settlement', with concessions made in return for social peace and in response to the high expectations of those who fought the war in hope of a better future. Since the latter part of the last century the state has been sensitive to the potential of the organized working class for undermining capitalism. It has recognized the need for welfare measures to defuse discontent and secure allegiance to the social order. In the words of Quintin Hogg: 'if you don't give the people reform, they are going to give you social revolution'.[20]

The Role of Enlightened Reformers

The socially aware middle class has also been instrumental in advocating and initiating welfare measures. The activities of social investigators in the nineteenth century and the Fabian Society in particular were significant. The flavour of the time is caught by George Sims writing about the life of the poor in 1889 and urging welfare legislation:

> It [the casual poor] has now got into a condition in which it cannot be left. This mighty mob of famished, deseased and filthy helots is getting dangerous, physically, morally, politically dangerous. The barriers which have kept it back are rotten and giving way and it may do the state a mischief if it be not looked to in time. Its fevers and its filth may spread to the homes of the wealthy; its lawless armies may sally forth and give us the taste of the lesson the mob has tried to teach now and again in Paris, when long years of neglect have done their work.[21]

In this context factions of the middle and upper classes, particularly among the professions, pressed for more active state machinery to meet the consequences of unrestrained capitalist development, to curb the activities of some sections of the ruling class and to avert social unrest, degeneration of the workforce and decay of the cities. The reformer's motivation was not solely altruistic concern for the condition of the working class but also recognition of the importance of such reforms for the very survival and growth of capitalism. The enlightened middle class urged manufacturers and industrialists to recognize 'the true interests of their own order'.[22]

The Contradictory Nature of Reform

In view of the complex history of the welfare state it is not surprising that we find that individual reforms contain contradictory elements. Marx devoted considerable attention to the Factory Acts and commentators have used his work as a classic illustration of the contradictory nature of reform.[23] Marx noted that these Acts were the outcome of a struggle by the working class, with support from the landed aristocracy and middle class. They represented a significant modification of the capitalist social system and benefited the workers, recognizing them as human beings and setting limits on the extent of their exploitation. Because the legislation was part of the capitalist state, the machinery for its enforcement was ineffective, reducing its impact on ruling-class interests. Marx noted that the legislation also benefited capitalism in two ways. By restricting exploitation it helped to produce a healthier, stronger workforce; by forcing the collapse of small, inefficient businesses, it rationalized the forces of production, hastening the re-structuring and concentration of capital.

Similarly other welfare reforms cannot be viewed simply as providing gains for working people. For example, unemployment benefits prevent starvation and acute poverty for those without a job. Because they are administered by a capitalist state this is done in a manner oppressive and demeaning to claimants. Unemployment benefits service capitalism by ensuring that the workforce is not debilitated whilst unemployed during recession and remains fit to return to work when needed. By mitigating the effects of unemployment, the state defuses it as an issue for class struggle. For a similar treatment of housing policy readers should turn to Ginsburg.[24]

Welfare in Service of Capital

We will examine the ways in which welfare state activity in general helps to preserve and promote the capitalist economic system.

Integration and Consensus

State initiatives on welfare help to channel the aspirations of working people through state institutions and bring them into a close relationship with the state. Winston Churchill, commenting on the benefits of national insurance, said:

> The idea is to increase the stability of our institutions by giving the mass of industrial workers a direct interest in maintaining them. With a 'stake' in the country in the form of insurance against evil days these workers will pay no attention to the vague promises of revolutionary socialism . . . it will make him a better citizen, a more efficient worker and a happier man.[25]

Welfare is a means of bringing in those who are potentially disaffacted and promotes the view of a caring society which cherishes its citizens. Although contradicted in everyday experience of welfare services, the impact of this ideology is powerful. People are really led to believe that they are cossetted by the welfare state.

Reproduction of the Labour Force

Welfare provision makes a crucial contribution to this important state activity. The significance of this task was crudely, but honestly, spelt out by Balfour:

> It is a most intolerable thing that we should permit the permanent deterioration of those who are fit for really good work. Putting aside all consideration of morals, all those considerations which move us as men of feeling, as flesh and blood, and looking at it with the hardest heart

and the most calculating eye, is it not very poor economy to scrap good machinery?[26]

The National Health Service, school milk and meals, and medical inspection of children all help to ensure a healthy workforce. Health campaigns, such as the one against smoking, can be understood in the same way and indeed one index of a significant health problem is the number of days' work lost through that condition. Education services, too, are geared to meeting the particular needs of capitalism and recent debates on curriculum content reflect this.[27]

Reproduction of Capitalist Social Relations

As well as being fit the workforce needs to be motivated to work, prepared to accept the discipline of labour and constraints of authority in the work place. The education system is the primary agent in moulding children into shape ready for labour.[28] However, other welfare agencies also have a significant role to play. For example, the benefits system is organized to emphasize the importance of work. Payment is contingent upon registering for work and the discipline of fortnightly signing (unless the claimant is deemed unexploitable because old, infirm, or a single mother). Leaving work voluntarily or being sacked for indiscipline are penalized by suspension of benefits, as is a refusal of suitable work offered. Levels of benefit are calculated to be lower than wages and the system reinforces the sexual relationships of capitalism – women's dependence on men – for example by the cohabitation rule.[29]

Welfare, Women and the Family

In carrying out these functions for capitalism the welfare state works not only through institutions such as hospitals and DHSS offices but also through what is thought of as a private institution – the family. Whilst the family remains the primary source of love, affection, care and concern for most people, the state has long recognized its important role in producing the future labour force, maintaining the current one and inculcating appropriate values. Social policy measures such as family allowances, tax relief and child benefit payments have been aimed at strengthening the family. Social work intervention (particularly since the Seebohm reorganization) is family-focused, seeking to improve the functioning of weak or 'problem' families. When social policy focuses on the family, the spotlight falls on women for it is they who usually bear the burden of responsibility for ensuring that the male workforce is fed, clothed, healthy and that children grow up to take their place in the factory. Elizabeth Wilson points out:

> The present economic crisis makes life even harder for women, whether working or not, for they must work harder in the home to make the same money go further, and they must bear the brunt of slashed welfare provisions. Hospital patients prematurely returned home to convalesce, elderly parents denied meals on wheels or home helps, children on half time schooling, unemployed husbands for that matter, all require more attention from Mother.[30]

It is the woman who is the focus of social work attention, whose budgeting, home care, discipline or handling of the children needs to improve.[31]

Welfare – Coercion and Consent

The welfare state plays a primary ideological role in securing consent, leading people to believe that our social system is both natural and just. First, the very existence of welfare services reassures people that 'something is being done', that people are looked after in society – the 'cradle to the grave' theme. Second, the state form in which services are delivered educates people about their position, appropriate sexual role and the importance of discipline and respect for authority. Third, its focus on the family reinforces sexual stereotypes and points to the family as the appropriate living unit.

In its operation, the welfare state works mostly with the consent of its consumers but if this cannot be secured then coercive measures are used. For example, in the field of education, school attendance is usually automatic. Parents send their kids to school because that is 'normal' and in their own best interests. But if children or parents withdraw consent then court proceedings are instigated, and thus coercive measures are pursued through the use of law.

THE LEGAL–JURIDICAL SYSTEM

We now examine that part of the state which has particular relevance for probation officers. We take the legal–juridical system (which we shall shorten to the juridical system) to include the law and its administration, crime, the courts, the police, prisons and, of course, the probation service. Our analysis locates the juridical system within the theory of the state already outlined. Law is a particularly important function of the state because it embodies the set of rules by which society is organized. It is a function shrouded in myths of independence and neutrality, so we will start by adopting a historical approach which illuminates links between the law and the ruling class.

Law – A Historical Perspective

Recent studies have shown that the eighteenth and nineteenth centuries were a period of rapid law-making when the basis of modern law, wedded to property, emerged. First the landed aristocracy and then the owners of industrial and finance capital shaped the law to protect their own interests. We start with an example from Marx's own work. In the fifteenth century most of this country's population were peasants, working both their own land and on the large estates of their feudal masters. They had rights to large areas of common land, providing them with timber, firewood, turf and grazing rights. With the expansion of cloth manufacturing the price of wool rose and the feudal lords took to raising sheep, usurped the common land, drove the peasantry from the land and depopulated the countryside unrestrained by tradition or law. In the law-making epoch this robbery was legalized by 'Bills for the Inclosure of Commons' which Marx describes as: 'decrees by which the landowners granted themselves the people's land as private property, decrees of expropriation of the people'. Between 1801 and 1831, 3,511,770 acres of common land were presented to landlords through the agency of Parliament. The consequence of this 'legal' appropriation was that the people's use of common lands became legally prohibited and punishable under the law. Property rights were transformed in favour of the dominant class and those new property rights were enshrined in law which reified them, lending them legitimacy.[32]

Social historians tell us that as the law developed it was increasingly concerned with preserving the property rights of the powerful and even followed the changing nature of property. When paper money and the banking system developed, fraud and forgery were made crimes. As new laws were made, the death penalty was routinely included as the sanction for infringing property rights. As a national and international market in food developed, there were local shortages of supply; food riots developed as a form of popular protest by the starving poor and the death penalty was extended to food rioters. Hay comments that

> the class that controlled Parliament was using the criminal sanction to enforce . . . the radical redefinition of property which gentlemen were making in their own interests during the eighteenth century.

He concludes:

> The law defined and maintained the bounds of power and wealth, and when we ask who controlled the criminal law, we see a familiar constellation: monarchy, aristocracy, gentry and, to a lesser extent, the great merchants.[33]

These crystal-clear links with ruling-class property rights have now receded into the base structure of modern law, becoming less visible and self-evident.[34]

The Juridical System – A Degree of Independence

We have pointed to a period when the juridical system was acting in a way directly expressive of the interests of landed capital. Commenting on that period, Hall *et al.* say:

> the arbitrary, openly class nature of the law . . . reflected the limited basis of the consent and participation which sustained . . . the emergent agrarian capitalist state.

They continue:

> the wider the political foundations of the state, the stronger the presence of the great 'unenfranchised' classes in it, the more – slowly and unevenly, to be sure – the law, in its routine operations, is driven towards a formal separation from the direct play of the class interests of the . . . ruling class.[35]

In our analysis of the state, we argued that it has a degree of independence, as a consequence of class struggle and because that meets the long-term needs of capital. Two centuries of political class struggle have similarly had their effect on the law and the juridical system has also developed 'relative autonomy'.

How does this coincide with the needs of capital? We have argued that the appearance of 'the neutral state' relies on forms of impersonal authority which mask real inequalities and cited 'the rule of law' as one such form. The modern capitalist state seeks to win consent, for only then can the state exact both obligation and obedience. It is crucial therefore to the interests of capital that the law appears as a universal norm, operating above class interests. Great stress is placed on the impartial 'rule of law' and on the formal 'separation of powers' (judicial from legislative, as taught in British Constitution lessons). Capital's long-term interests have required a progressive autonomization of the law, even though this could act against immediate ruling-class interests. This gradual and uneven process has produced 'a degree of judicial "space" which the working class sometimes appropriate for their own defence and protection'.[36] The 'relative autonomy' of the law tends to conceal its class character but does not remove it.

Law – In Service of Capital

The law is an important carrier of ideology and we return to this role later. Here we identify three ways in which the juridical system works directly in the interests of capital.

In Defence of Property

Although times have changed since the eighteenth century, the law, both civil and criminal, is still above all concerned with property. We will concentrate on the criminal law and simply note that the foundations of civil law lie in the central relations of capitalism – property and the contract – and this is reflected in its forms and procedure.[37] The criminal law demarcates illegal forms of property appropriation and damage to property. So, for example, burglary, fraud, theft, criminal damage and trespass are prohibited. In the same process, other forms of property appropriation and damage are legitimized. Tax avoidance, for example, is both permitted and encouraged with some accountants fully employed uncovering new loopholes. The pollution of the environment in the pursuit of capital accumulation or war is not censured. The extraction of surplus value is seen as a legal and creditworthy activity – the maximization of profits is just good business. The law disallows those methods of property accumulation which threaten the present distribution of wealth. The illegality of theft is absolute – dishonesty is dishonesty – and so trivial matters are processed with the full ceremony of the law. Readers will be able to add to our recollections of a man sent to prison for stealing a bottle of milk, a juvenile charged with a first offence of handling a stolen tennis ball and a man charged with theft of an onion, dug up from a field. Hay gives historical perspective. An ancient civil doctrine decreed that a starving man had the right to steal enough food to keep himself for a week. In the eighteenth century legal authorities rejected this doctrine because 'it was impossible to admit poverty as a legal defence without wholly eroding the property statute'.[38] Any weakening of the principle that the criminal law is absolute threatens to undermine the sanctity of property.

The 'rule of law' applies to all and the juridical system sometimes imposes its authority on 'illegal' capitalist transactions. However, the administration of justice is not so even-handed – the treatment offenders receive often reflects their relationship to property. One example will suffice to make our point. On 13 June 1980, John Stonehouse was driven away from the bankruptcy court in a silver Rolls-Royce after being granted a discharge from his £816,000 criminal bankruptcy. He had offered £4–£5 a week towards paying off his creditors but, hearing that Stonehouse's only income was a £58 per week pension from Parliament, this was turned down by the Official Receiver, who said: 'I do not want to discourage you in making an offer but my experience tells me that, with the medical stress to which you may be put, to find £4/£5 a week may be difficult. And it is not going to make very much difference one way or the other'.[39]

This highlights the difference between bankruptcy procedure, even criminal bankruptcy, and the way in which working-class debts are handled. The attitude to Stonehouse's offer will contrast sharply with probation officers' experience of the way courts approach fine and compensation enforcement, by ordering large weekly payments backed by resort to imprisonment.[40]

In Reproducing Social Relations

Another function of the law and its administration is to reinforce and strengthen the social relations which exist under capitalism. Here we concentrate on two examples: sexual relations and the relations of production.

It is implicit in the law that women are regarded as the property of either their husband or father. The severe penalties attached to rape are a punishment for the defilement of another man's property, rather than simply a form of protection for women. It is at present legally impossible for a man to be guilty of raping his wife, because it is assumed in law that he has free access to her, regardless of her will. Another example lies in the apparent contradiction that women who solicit for prostitution are prosecuted, while their male customers are not. That injustice rests on the tenet that women's sexuality is to be confined to marriage and the home, while men's sexuality is permitted wider expression.[41]

The law reinforces the relations of capitalist production. For example, it endorses the employer/employee relationship as one of a freely made contract and equal exchange, thus legitimating the extraction of surplus value and an exploitative relationship. The courts deal severely with any activity that threatens that relationship. One of the authors witnessed the following illustration in a magistrates' court in 1976. A defendant pleaded guilty to theft. He worked as a despatch clerk in a cheese warehouse and was discovered to have sent out £1,000 worth of cheese but only invoiced the retailer for £500, splitting the profit with him. His employers were shocked – he had worked there for 30 years and was their most trusted employee. He was sacked and in court the magistrate delivered a 'sermon' on breach of trust. The police, in giving his antecedents, revealed that he was earning £30 per week, his wife had been forced to give up work following a stroke and he was struggling to meet his mortgage repayments. The man, without previous convictions, was given a suspended prison sentence and ordered to compensate his employers. Another example of the connection between law and the relation of production can be seen in drug offences which are 'crimes without victims'. Jock Young has suggested that some forms of drug use have been declared illegal because of the hedonistic values they

represent and the danger this creates for the preservation of
the work ethic and its corollary, earned leisure.[42]

In Preserving Public Order

The law is also concerned with the preservation of a society
in which the accumulation of capital can continue
smoothly. Hall *et al.* say that it 'secures in moments of open
class confrontation just that stability and cohesion without
which the steady reproduction of capital and the unfolding
of capitalist relations would be a far more hazardous and
unpredictable affair'.[43] The law as a set of rules preserves
order in a general sense, delineating appropriate conduct
and encouraging conformity by imposing sanctions on
those who break the rules. Beyond this general sense, the
law includes a series of public order measures designed to
keep in check protests or actions which might be a potential
threat to capitalism. For example, the Public Order Act 1936
gives the police the power to enforce a blanket ban on public
demonstrations (routinely used to stop demonstrations
during 1981). Such law responds quickly to developments in
class struggle. For instance, as economic recession set in
during the early 1970s, and business started to collapse,
factory occupation emerged as a working-class tactic in
fighting closures. This was countered first by innovative
judicial interpretations in the civil courts and then
criminalized by Part Two of the Criminal Law Act 1977
(Criminal Trespass), which also sought to outlaw squatting,
and protest occupations of buildings. Similarly, the
Thatcher government's determination to restrict the right to
picket can be understood as an attempt to outlaw interruptions of capital accumulation. Commenting on the Thatcher
government, Ralph Miliband emphasizes this important
role of the law:

> The government's economic strategy is a rag-bag of
> hopes, hunches, prejudices and dogmas. But it does
> have a coherent *social* strategy which is designed to
> produce a 'social climate' favourable to capitalist enter-

prise. . . . An important element in the government's social strategy is the erosion by legislative means (and in due course by judicial and coercive means) of the right to strike.[44]

The Contradictory Effect of Law

We have shown that the law performs important tasks on behalf of capital but earlier argued that to do so effectively, the juridical system has developed a degree of independence and sought to raise laws to the level of universal norms. Consequently the law must at times 'police' capitalism and enforce sanctions against irregular capitalist transactions. Many business dodges narrowly elude the criminal law but some companies are prosecuted, although regulations affecting commercial concerns are unenthusiastically enforced. Occasionally individuals are singled out for exemplary treatment, as in recent corruption cases involving John Poulson, T. Dan Smith and others. Invariably these are portrayed as isolated incidents of individual excesses – 'the unacceptable face of capitalism' – rather than its routine operation. In contrast the working class feels the full weight of the law, is policed, arrested, fills the courts and prisons, and is placed on probation.

Working class people have a contradictory experience of the law because it does afford them some protection to life and limb, and for their small amounts of property. The working class, too, can call the police if burgled or assaulted and the complaint will receive attention. Even when up against the law, the working class has certain 'rights under the law' which, although limited and sometimes arbitrarily denied, are considerably better than no rights at all. Civil liberties, such as jury trial and habeas corpus, are worth protecting against attack even though they are in themselves 'fetishized forms', conveying an image of equality and absolute rights.

Through struggle the working class has also won rights as a series of exemptions from the common law: 'The rights to organise, to combine, to withdraw labour and to picket are rights, established only by means of a brutal and extended struggle, which set some minimal exceptions to the rights of property against labour'.[45] Such rights are fragile and under continual attack by the state. A recent example of class struggle around the law was the fight by the trades unions against the 1971 Industrial Relations Act, which was eventually repealed.[46]

The Ideological Role of Law

The various parts of the state apparatus play not only a direct role in supporting capital, but also an important ideological role. They maintain a framework of reference so that the 'way things are' is seen by people as 'common sense' and the boundaries of debate are circumscribed. The law is a powerful carrier of ideology and here we look at four aspects of its role.

The Law as a Fetishized Form

We have shown that fundamentally the law is rooted in the class division in society, yet has the appearance of being neutral and impartial, acting above sectional interests. This image is supported by the way its rituals set it apart and its technical language and procedures render it a field for experts. The law is a fetishized form and its appearance of universality gives it an important role as a 'bedrock metaphor of social harmony and consensus'.[47] Breaches of the law thus mean more than a simple infraction of the rules: they are taken to indicate an attack on the whole fabric of society. The criminalization of an activity by the state is an extremely powerful sanction and its effect is dramatic.

The Law and the Individual

The law deals only with the individual citizen who is seen as an abstract subject with certain legal rights but also certain obligations. The assumption of individual personal responsibility is a cornerstone of the criminal law, so that, for instance, ignorance of a statute is no defence. In the courts, society is reduced to an atomized mass of individual citizens. Each case is prosecuted as though it had no connection with any other and is divorced from its social context. The limits of relevant evidence are tightly drawn to exclude such connections. In this way class interests, property relations and common causes are obscured. This feature of the juridical system has an ideological effect – crime is seen only as the product of individual weakness or wickedness, setting the offender apart from society and legitimating the work of the criminal justice system.[48]

The Law as Educator

The law and its administration have a crucial educative role. The law is administered in public, breaches of the law are treated in a ritualized manner in the courts, are extremely visible and exhaustively reported in local and national media. The act of sentencing provides judges and magistrates with an opportunity to deliver 'sermons' from the bench, designed not so much to influence the offender but rather for public consumption. They are intended to teach others the dangers of breaking the law, to communicate definitions of unacceptable behaviour and to reassure the public that the state is fulfilling its undertaking to maintain social order. Hall *et al.*, in a detailed study of 'mugging', demonstrate clearly the way in which judges play a major role in forming public opinion about crime.[49]

The Law and Mercy

The use of mercy plays an important part in the operation of the law. Once again Hay's historical analysis helps us to understand its role. In the eighteenth century the death penalty applied to many crimes but the number of executions carried out was limited and a large number of pardons were granted. Hay demonstrates that the system for obtaining pardons depended on petitioners proving their respectability and this involved a complex appeal through the existing system of power and patronage. So the application of mercy reinforced political and social power, producing and renewing bonds of obligation. Hay says: 'Discretion allowed a prosecutor to terrorise the petty thief and then command his gratitude, or at least the approval of his neighbour as a man of compassion'.[50] The courts no longer deal in death and terror but we can see parallels with the situation Hay describes. Mercy is an important element in sentencing; it is used to encourage behaviour and provides a humane veneer to the harsh penal process. Thus mercy helps to maintain public support for the criminal justice system.

The Law – Coercion and Consent

The juridical system is usually described in marxist analysis as the repressive state apparatus and it is clear that the police, arrest, detention, the courts and imprisonment do form the routine coercive operation of the state. In other parts of the state apparatus, the coercive side is more hidden and only emerges when consent fails, usually by invoking the law. Whilst recognizing this clear distinction between the juridical system and other parts of the state, it is important to remember that the process of 'routine coercion' is supported by widespread consent amongst the population. In discussing the 'relative autonomy', the contradictory nature and ideological role of law, we have identified the factors which help to secure this consent. History reveals that without consent the criminal justice system cannot function smoothly; in the past juries have refused to convict, and victims declined to prosecute, when they have believed penalties to be too harsh; in the eighteenth century hangings were disrupted and 'rescues' effected.[51] Such reactions bring the law into disrepute, so it is essential to the state that consent is maintained.

In our discussion of the theory of the state we introduced the idea of 'coercive tilt', when consensus begins to break down and the state responds by increased use of coercive measures in an attempt to restore social harmony around a respect for authority and the need for discipline, an 'authoritarian consensus'.[52] We would argue that current demands for 'law and order' mark such a tilt. Hall *et al*. have provided a detailed study of an early manifestation of this development in their work on 'mugging'. They show that concern about 'mugging' in the early 1970s was dispropor- tionate to any change in its incidence and suggest that it was the theme for a 'moral panic' spread by police reactions, judicial statements and sensational media reporting. This produced raised public awareness, then alarm about crime generally. In this way the ground was prepared for public acceptance of 'law and order' developments. 'Mugging' and similar panics around terrorism, race, scroungers, pickets, militants and juvenile delinquents have combined to create a major shift in the public debate on crime and law enforcement.

Appeals for 'law and order' connect with real fears experienced by working people but these are fuelled by the juridical system and the media. The state attempts in this way to produce managed consent for the coercive tilt already under way. In this process the state adopts a risky strategy because failure to manage consent can lead to a reaction against increased coercion and a further with- drawal of support. This can be seen in the recent growth of some public concern about Special Patrol Groups, deaths in police custody and MUFTI Squads in prison.

Crime is consistently presented as one of society's biggest problems. Jock Young captures its importance:

> Crime control is a central part of the legitimation of the state, and the element of reality contained in such control underlies the process of *ideological inversion*. That is, to the question, 'why does capitalism have severe problems?' the answer is 'because of problems such as crime' and not that capitalism is the cause of such problems.[53]

Support is given to the state because it is seen to be dealing with the major problem of crime. The strong measures the state adopts to deal with crime are thereby legitimated and so are available to be used against other 'enemies of the state'.[54]

Prison – The Ultimate Expression of Law

In the next chapter we examine the probation service in the light of our analysis. Space precludes a similarly detailed study of all the different components of the criminal justice system but the role of prisons requires some particular attention because it underpins the whole juridical system and is the final repository of the forces of coercion. As George Jackson put it: 'The ultimate expression of law is not order – it's prison. We have hundreds upon hundreds of prisons, and thousands upon thousands of laws, yet there is no social order, no social peace'.[55] Imprisonment means loss of liberty, of civil rights and the potential exercise of authority over practically every aspect of existence. Its symbolic value is enormous, representing all that is bad and evil. Prison buildings are forbidding and stark. Secrecy about what goes on in prisons strengthens fantasies and fears in the public mind. It is understood that prison is where you go if you break the rules and is to be avoided.

There is no developed marxist analysis of prison but Foucault's book *Discipline and Punish: The Birth of the Prison* has some elements of a marxist perspective and offers useful insights. Foucault analysed the role of prison as a place for reform. The introduction of the rehabilitative aim in imprisonment was coincident with the development of capitalism. The purpose of deprivation of liberty became 'transformation' – producing the obedient citizen, by what Foucault called 'the disciplinary process'. He argues that this process remains the basis of our prisons and identifies its main components as hierarchical surveillance and the measurement of the individual against a norm to be achieved. Power is exercised through knowledge of the individual; observation and documentation turn each individual into a case. Foucault notes that the need for this type of disciplinary power arises with the growth of a capitalist economy and suggests it is used in a variety of institutions (factories, schools, hospitals, etc.) but approaches its ideal type in prisons. There seems to be some parallel between Foucault's 'disciplinary process' and the marxist concept of 'the reproduction of capitalist social relations'.

Foucault identifies the consequences of the 'disciplinary process' for prison regimes – the classification of inmates, work and education as the means of transformation, social and medical staff to supervise that process, adjustment of the sentence according to progress and the provision of supervision and assistance on release. All these features are aimed at the transformation of the prisoner into a useful citizen.

That the prison manifestly fails to achieve its given task of producing obedient citizens, or normalizing those who are imprisoned, is not of great importance. The values of capitalism are promoted in their strictest form within the prison through the disciplinary process. Although actually ineffective on an individual basis, the prison serves as a prototype for the capitalist value system. Setting prison inmates apart provides a symbolic confirmation of the difference between them – the delinquents – and us, 'the law-abiding citizens'.

Foucault notes that the prison is an institution of 'extreme solidity', a permanent feature of our social landscape. Because it represents more than just locking up offenders, it is a difficult institution to change or remove. He suggests two conditions which might bring this about: if the prison outlived its symbolic value or if the disciplinary function of the prison could be transferred to other agencies. Foucault calls this 'the growth of the disciplinary networks' and names some agencies beginning to take on the functions of the prison – medicine, psychology, education, public assistance and social work. To this list we add the probation service.[56]

7
Probation:
A Marxist Analysis

In this chapter, we analyse the probation service as part of the state apparatus we have outlined, using the same theoretical framework to identify the ways in which the probation service is supportive of the capitalist social order. We hope to overcome limitations in the radical critique of probation by refining and developing its marxist analysis, by developing a perspective on the role and relative contribution of probation within the state apparatus and by relating our analysis more closely to specific probation tasks.

By understanding probation in this way, it is possible to grasp the significance of the pressures, confusions and tensions of the probation officer's job, described in Part I. Because we will be identifying the structural position and role of the service, the connections we make will largely be with what we described as the official account of the job – what probation officers are supposed to do, not what they actually do. We return to the practice account later in the chapter when we look at resistance to, and struggle within, those structural constraints. Our first task is to locate the probation service in relation to the major state systems we have considered.

PROBATION – A SMALL COG IN THE JURIDICAL MACHINE

Some writers exhibit an alarming tendency to treat the probation service as a 'world apart' with its own philosophy, values and aims. We concentrate instead on its interconnectedness with, and dependence upon, larger and more powerful institutions. Probation work can be related to both the major state systems studied in the last chapter – the welfare state and the juridical apparatus.

The radical view of probation has emphasized its similarity to social work and generic training stresses common factors. This can underplay connections to the juridical system with serious practical consequences – for instance, if a probation officer recommends against probation on social work grounds, such as lack of need or motivation, the court may impose a harsher sentence. Much of modern social work practice involves links with the juridical apparatus or state systems raising similar issues, so what we are pointing out is not so much a distinction as a necessary but commonly neglected context. The personal social services can be identified as a small part of welfare state provision offering some benefits and services to working-class people, although in a contradictory way. Radicals have tended to view probation, too, as part of the welfare state. Although the service has a distinct welfare orientation in many aspects of its work and probation officers are in regular contact with welfare services, it plays an extremely small role in the direct provision of material benefits to clients. Its traditional and continuing concern has rather been with, using Foucault's term, the transformation of the offender. [1] While connections and parallels with welfare services can be seen, we think it is more useful and consistent to locate the probation service primarily in the general context of the juridical system.

Close and significant links are readily identifiable. Not only are probation officers in everyday contact with other parts of the juridical system – particularly courts and prisons – but that system actively determines their work. The various probation tasks are directly related to the legal process and clients are almost exclusively drawn from the people defined as criminal by the juridical system. Not only the 'who' but the 'how' is determined – reports are prepared when requested by courts or prisons, the courts decide

whether an offender is placed on probation, made subject to
a community service order, or whether the service's involvement will be offering after-care following a prison
sentence. Because most of its functions are secondary
adjuncts to the legal process, the operational definitions of
the probation service are established by the juridical
apparatus. This means that the service necessarily upholds
the values inherent in the law. Here are just a few examples:
because the law is primarily concerned with property
offences, most probationers have been convicted of dishonesty; because the law bears most heavily on the working
class, the probation service clientele is overwhelmingly
working class; and because individualization is a fundamental feature of the law it similarly dominates probation
work.

Beyond these broad determinants, the juridical apparatus imposes constraints on the way in which probation
officers work. Two examples illustrate this point. In our
examination of social enquiry work in Part I, we pointed out
the way in which the content, structure and orientation of
reports is affected by the probation officer's need to retain
credibility – the court's 'limits of relevance' are largely
accepted and even recommendations are tailored to the
court's own inclinations. Similarly, in examining prison
welfare work, we demonstrated that it assumed a servicing
role within the prison's routine and that, far from representing an 'oppositional presence', was readily incorporated in the general task of the prison.

These intimate and extensive connections make it
essential to locate the probation service within the context
of the juridical system. This assists in appreciating the
significance of its tasks and role within the state apparatus.
This understanding of the probation service's role as part
of, and in harmony with, the overall role of the juridical
apparatus also helps us to put into perspective some of the
new developments in the probation service. One of
Foucault's conditions for the removal of prisons was the
growth in the community of the same type of disciplinary
control that exists in prison[2] – 'control in the community'.

Thus, in order to be acceptable, 'alternatives to custody' must seek to fulfil the same functions as imprisonment. We pointed out in discussing new developments how the probation service is under pressure to accept new orders and licences, containing more specific and stricter conditions and has been developing facilities which extend the supervisory contact between client and probation officer.

PROBATION – IN SERVICE OF CAPITAL

In the last chapter we analysed both the general functions of the state and the particular contribution of the law in supporting the capitalist social system. Now we identify the way in which many of these functions are echoed in the particular tasks of the probation service, drawing on our examination of those tasks in Part I. Although probation operates within the general framework provided by the juridical system, it also performs a particular role as the 'welfare arm' of the coercive state apparatus. We noted earlier that although the law's appearance of 'universality' obscured real inequalities, the juridical system did have a degree of independence from the direct play of class interests. The probation service takes on that same degree of independence but this is amplified in practice for two reasons. First, its specific brief to act as the welfare arm of the system allows more weight to be given to the interests of the offender. Second, the necessary discretion given to the probation officer allows more flexibility of approach. Probation officers commonly regard their own work as value free, an attitude encouraged by the 'universality' of professionalism. Probation work, like a wide range of state activities, seeks, through professionalism, a detached, objective, 'scientific' appearance of 'expert competence' which parallels the appearance of 'neutrality' assumed by the law. We will demonstrate that nevertheless the values of capitalism underpin the work of the service in both direct and ideological functions. We now consider the contribution of the probation service in reproducing capitalist social relations, in individualizing crime, in promoting integration and consensus in society and in introducing important elements of mercy and discretion to the juridical system.

Reproduction of Capitalist Social Relations

This important part of the state's activity makes possible the continuation of capitalism by ensuring the provision of a labour force with the necessary skills, attitudes and motivation. Delinquency has been theorized as the failure of the family to reproduce capitalist social relations[3] and it is clear that the purpose of most penal policy is the teaching of those relations – what Foucault calls 'producing the obedient citizen'.[4] In chapter 3 we showed how the Prison Rules and official rhetoric about prisons embody this purpose. The same sentiments permeate the work of the probation service and we identify five main aims.

Promoting Conformity

Probation officers are explicitly and implicitly required to encourage their clients to live within the law. Probation orders, parole and other licences all impose the moral imperative that the subject 'be of good behaviour' and this means more than simply avoiding offences. Probation is intended to influence offenders to accept and conform to their place in society. The same value is evident in the newer developments – in many probation hostels, for instance, although they now deal with adults, a curfew is set to encourage a regulated and work-oriented life style. In various forms the probation service promotes conformity and discourages dissent, thus supporting the social order of capitalism.

Encouraging Work

One of the conditions of probation, repeated in other licences, requires the offender to 'lead an industrious life'. The Probation Rules clarify that this means 'suitable and regular employment'[5] and probation officers find themselves encouraging and cajoling clients into becoming part of the workforce. Occasionally clients are breached for failing to find work.[6] Amongst the newer developments, the day training centres are heavily oriented towards employment, so that Elizabeth Burney questions: 'Is it right, for instance, to lay emphasis on job-finding in a time of increasing unemployment, especially in areas like South Wales?'[7] Stuart Palmer, in his study of hostels, notes that so much emphasis was placed on work that residents had to be off the premises during the day, even if not working. Paradoxically this may encourage offences and so defeat the main object of hostel provision.[8] Amongst the newer social work methods, social skills training is most often used in connection with employment. Efforts are made to enhance clients' skills so that they can compete in the job market. Attention is also paid to the employer–employee relationship, in which clients are encouraged to accept authority in the workplace. Ironically, as unemployment soars, we have shown that new developments in the probation service have become increasingly work-oriented.

In some respects then the probation service plays a direct role in equipping clients to join the workforce and in all its activities pressurizes them to work, often with little regard to the degree of exploitation they will encounter. The commitment of the probation service to the work ethic goes beyond a mere recognition of the imperative of capitalism – the need to sell your labour to survive – to an enthusiastic endorsement of the capitalist relations of production.

Accepting Authority

The authority of the probation officer over the client is implicit in all forms of supervision. Thus, for example, the subject of a Borstal licence must visit the probation officer or receive visits at home as directed. Failure to comply with this or any other condition of supervision can lead to recall to Borstal. Probation officers are expected to represent the acceptable face of authority to their clients and thus encourage a general acceptance of, and compliance with, authority. Some new developments – by, for instance, requiring attendance at a day centre or workshop – extend that authority over wider areas of the client's life.

We have shown that features of the state form, such as hierarchy and bureaucracy, are an important part of capitalist social relations because they organize and maintain the structures necessary for discipline. The acceptance of authority is a fundamental requirement and the relationship between probation officer and client reflects and promotes this need of the capitalist structure.

Using Leisure Constructively

Not only should these useful citizens produced by the probation officer be conforming, working and prepared to accept authority but they should also maintain themselves in a condition fit for labour. Constructive leisure activities are seen as important and are promoted by the probation service. The Probation Rules place a duty on probation officers to encourage the use of appropriate social, recreational and educational facilities. Day centres induce participants to extend their leisure activities by including hobbies and sports in their programmes. This emphasis is particularly strong in the service's work with younger clients where Intermediate Treatment and Outward Bound ventures are expanding activities. Even in community service it is argued that, through the work experience, participants will learn constructive uses of leisure in voluntary service with the disadvantaged.

These activities are reflections at one level of an old social work theme, 'clean air through dirty minds' or what Geoff Pearson described as 'sociological pastoral'.[9] They are intended to replace more hedonistic pastimes, such as excessive drinking or the use of drugs, which might interfere with the discipline of labour. They can also contribute to public order, keeping young people in particular 'off the streets'.[10]

Preserving Capitalist Sexual Relations

We have noted how other state agencies perpetuate and reinforce the subordinate role of women. The probation service works on the basis of formal equality between the sexes but mirrors the legal differentiation of sex role we have identified, such as the law on soliciting. In practice we can identify the same tendency. Unlike social work generally probation has a largely male clientele, except in the limited areas of juvenile and family work. However, what provision there is for women tends to reinforce and promote their position as wives or mothers and to focus on ways of improving their functioning within that role.[11] Through their work with male clients, probation officers indirectly express attitudes towards women which collude with conventional stereotypes. Probation officers, for example, view the acquisition of a wife or steady girlfriend as a means of cutting short a delinquent's career and bringing him into the domestic sphere. The support of girlfriends and wives is enlisted to keep an eye on the male client, to curb excessive drinking and to encourage contact with the probation officer. In this way, probation officers, often quite unconsciously, reinforce the role stereotype functional to capitalism.

Individualization

Our analysis in Part I showed that the concept of individualization is fundamental to the work of the probation service, and our subsequent examination of the state reveals it as a key feature of the state under capitalism. Within the juridical system particularly, the spotlight is on the individual and the purpose of the penal system, and the prison, is the 'transformation' of the individual into an obedient citizen. We can identify ways in which the probation service mirrors the features of Foucault's 'disciplinary process':[12] the caseload made up of 45 or so individual cases, emphasis on casework and the one-to-one relationship and, above all, probation records, which are used to document the personal details of each individual and the measurement of progress towards normality over time, by both the running record (Part C) and quarterly summaries (Part B).

Individualization within the probation service can also be understood as an example of a fetishized form. We have noted that this is a characteristic feature of capitalism: a surface appearance conceals a fundamental inequality. Social work generally rests on a belief in the importance of respect for the uniqueness of the individual. So clients are handled separately, the differentness of each is explored and individual programmes of treatment are devised. This focus on the individual all but obscures the class issues involved in the law and its enforcement – for example the unequal distribution of wealth, the way the law bears heavily on working-class dishonesty and the effects of discriminatory policing. This concentration on differentness hides common causes and redirects possibilities for collective action into the search for individual solutions.

The cherished one-to-one probation officer/client relationship can also be understood as a fetishized form. It is portrayed as containing an element of equality between the two parties – the client consents and shares in working out aims and ways of achieving them. In a currently fashionable development in social work, this is raised to the level of that principal capitalist form, the 'contract'. Yet, like the wage contract, at the root of the probation relationship lies a fundamental inequality in power, disguised in everyday probation practice.

Integration and Consensus

The probation service, like the welfare state, plays an important role in the capitalist state in promoting consensus. First, as we noted in Part I, the role of the probation service is to 'bring in' those individuals who have put themselves outside society by breaking the law. The probation officer helps the offender to fit back into society: 'offers him the help of society in adjusting his conduct to its demands. . . . The offender is conditionally entrusted with freedom so that he may learn the social duties it involves'.[13] Volunteers – representatives of the caring community – are enlisted to befriend the offender and help in this integrative task. The client who carries out community service is seen as re-paying a debt to the community incurred by breaking the law, and so can be accepted back into society. A core concept of probation work is the integration of the offender within society, thus enlarging the consensus.

The second integrative aspect of the probation service is its wider role as promoter of the image of a humane, caring society. In Part I we identified probation officer's work in the harsh penal system as a 'sop to the liberal conscience': by mitigating the worst it gives a veneer of care and con-cern. Similarly, by acting as 'the benevolent face of the penal system' it extends belief in welfare from 'the cradle to the grave' even to the court and prison cell. In this way the probation service helps to secure consent for the operation of the penal system. It has then an ideological role to play in promoting the view of a caring consensus society, one in which those who break the law are both looked after and given a second chance, so that they can be brought back into the community.

Exercise of Mercy and Discretion

We have noted in our analysis of the juridical system that mercy and discretion play an important part in securing consent and the probation service's contribution to this is significant. The offender being placed on probation, rather than being imprisoned, can be understood as an act of mercy. It is, however, conditional on abiding by a set of requirements, and can be reversed if these are not adhered to. Similarly home leave and parole are conditional on requirements being fulfilled and appropriate behaviour in prison: they can be withdrawn if the offender's cooperation is not forthcoming. Probation officers are given consider-able discretion in carrying out supervision as a means of trying to engage the client's cooperation, since this is more effectively and usefully obtained by persuasion than by resort to coercive measures. The act of mercy places offenders under certain obligations and draws them into a continuing relationship with society's power structure.

This use of mercy helps to secure consent to the penal system on a wider basis. The penal system is seen as flexible, exceptions can be made, special circumstances taken into account. Potential opposition to the harshness of the system can be defused by reference to the possibility of mercy and discretion.

THE IDEOLOGICAL SIGNIFICANCE OF PROBATION

We have outlined the four main ways in which the probation service carries out its role as part of the state in the service of capitalism. It does not stand alone but must be seen as acting in conjunction with other parts of the state apparatus, many of which have a much larger role. It will be clear from our account that whilst the probation service is expected to contribute directly to the reproduction of capitalist social relations, much of its role is in the ideological rather than practical sphere. Like prisons, the probation service carries out important ideological functions for capital, even when its efforts are not directly effective in producing obedient citizens. The values and beliefs promoted and maintained by the probation service reflect those required for the capitalist system. The roles of individualization, integration and the promotion of consensus contribute to the maintenance of capitalist hegemony.

PROBATION – COERCION AND CONSENT

We have outlined the significance of the coercion/consent duality in our earlier discussion of the state and here use it to further our understanding of some aspects of probation. Our outline of the function of the probation service, particularly in the discussion of mercy, discretion and integration, showed that the probation service acts as a securer of consent to the penal system, the coercive apparatus of the state.

We can also use the coercion/consent duality to understand the tasks of the probation service. By and large, probation officers try to work with the consent of their clients – we have shown how this is made possible through the use of discretion. But coercive measures (recall, breach) back up all orders and licences. The threat of coercion underpins the probation officer/client relationship, is used to try to obtain cooperation (by for example the dispatching of warning letters) and may be invoked if all else fails. Resort to coercive measures runs the risk of total alienation of the individual concerned but can have an educative role for others.

Understanding the tasks of the service as a consent/coercion duality helps us to appreciate the care/control issue. We noted in Part I that an assumption underlying the work of the probation service was that care and control are compatible, but that some who took part in the care/control debates argued that the two are polar opposites. If we understand care and control as the consent/coercion duality, we can appreciate that their underlying purpose is the same, but that their particular modes of operation are very different. Probation officers engaged in the care/control debate tended then to be arguing about which ways of working are acceptable, consistent with clients' civil liberties, realistic, practical and most likely to retain the cooperation of the client. In accepting that coercion/consent or control/care have the same underlying purpose, we should not ignore the significance for both probation officers and clients of those different modes of operation.

Finally we noted in our analysis of the state, that a tilt towards coercion was underway in society and here we can identify some of the consequences for the probation service. We noted that one of the ways in which consent was secured was by appealing to the need for 'law and order' to deal with 'moral panics' in which crime is a major theme. This has a direct effect on the probation officers, who find sentencers affected by 'moral panics' and shifting to harsher sentences against arguments for mercy. The consequent rise in the prison population and the recent introduction of pilot 'short, sharp shock' regimes in two detention centres directly affect probation officers in their prison welfare and after-care tasks. The drift into a 'law and order' society has also produced proposals for change. These are characterized by the use of more, and tougher, conditions in probation orders, suggestions for increased use of breach proceedings and that probation officers should act as 'surveillance' agents, devoid of any social work role.[14] The general trend is towards the use of more coercive measures and greater restrictions on clients. The coercive tilt is likely to produce a harder probation service, servicing a harsher penal system.

PROBATION OFFICERS AS STATE SERVANTS

Our analysis has identified how the work of the probation service contributes to the state function. It also has implications for probation officers in their role as employees and we now examine some of the consequences of working within the state apparatus.

Carrier of State Values

Along with their jobs, state workers inherit the state's value-set, so probation officers find themselves representing laws, norms and beliefs which are functional to the state under capitalism but which they may not share. They have to defend and promote institutions, laws or principles which they may actively oppose for example – the prison system, the law on soliciting or cannabis, the value of work at any price, obedience to authority. Probation officers have to promote some values or activities, and censure others, whilst personally feeling little enthusiasm for those stands – for example encouraging the work ethic, condemning small thefts or DHSS frauds, disapproving of hedonistic leisure pursuits. So there may be tension between the demands of the job – respect the courts, believe in the consensus society and the value of reform – and the personal feelings of probation officers. In dealings with clients they often feel hypocritical, promoting values that they don't really believe in and recommending solutions which they would not adopt themselves.

Subject to the State Form

We have described how clients are subject to the hierarchical state form, under the authority of the probation officer. In the same way probation officers are part of a hierarchical structure of management which watches over their work through inspection of records, assessment and supervision. Probation officers supervise clients, and are themselves supervised by senior probation officers, who are themselves supervised.

In their daily work on behalf of clients probation officers have to cope with the bureaucratic state form in other agencies – trying to get through to the DHSS, hanging on the phone for ages trying to sort out a fuel bill, or never knowing who to speak to in the housing department to get a sensible answer.

Individualization

We have noted the significance of the focus on the individual under capitalism, how this 'fetishized form' masks fundamental inequalities and structural issues, and how this is translated into the probation officer/client relationship. In a similar manner we can identify the ways in which the individual probation officer is the focus of attention – through the division of labour in the probation service and the whole system of supervision and assessment. The problems and difficulties probation officers raise with their seniors meet with individualistic, psychologistic responses and structural constraints are ignored – the caseworker is caseworked!

Problems of an Oppositional Stance

We have outlined some areas in which probation officers may find themselves personally opposed to the values and institutions they are expected to represent. They find that they are both 'In and Against the State'.[15] But acting on that oppositional stance can present problems. Many of the probation officer's duties are set out in legislation and subject to the authority of such powerful institutions as courts and prisons, so that refusing them takes on more significance than a simple breach of contract. An oppositional stance in court can become a contempt of court and theoretically lead to imprisonment. An oppositional stance over prisons could lead to prosecution for breach of the Official Secrets Act, or expressed within the prison can result in arbitrary exclusion. In both settings a loss of credibility and influence is feared, as are the consequences of making a stand on the individual client. There is a danger that, in response to such fears, opposition becomes so muted that the probation officer becomes totally incorporated in the juridical system.

Recognition of such problems has given probation officers some understanding of the need for collective forms of action, mostly channelled through NAPO which affords some protection. Even this is not without problems. For all those working within the state it is difficult to take oppositional stances which strike at the state rather than having their major impact on the working class, who may benefit from services provided.

The Personal and the Political

We see many of the problems faced by probation officers as common to most state employees. However, we suggest that there is one added dimension in probation and social work requiring special comment. In comparison with other jobs, they call for a much closer engagement of the worker's own personality and feelings. The recruiting material for the probation service makes this clear:

The basis of the work lies in the personal relationship with the offender.

And recruits should be:

> mature, self-reliant individuals with stable personalities
> and a knowledge of their own strengths and weaknesses.
> They should have a healthy curiosity about what makes
> people behave as they do, and an ability to respond to
> them and make them feel at ease. They must also be
> patient listeners.[16]

These examples show that the use of the 'personal' is
expected to play a large part in probation work. The state
seeks to use personal attributes and qualities to carry out its
political work. It is not surprising that probation officers
often complain of 'feeling used'.

RESISTANCE IN PROBATION

So far we have concentrated on what probation officers are
supposed to do. In Part I we presented practice accounts
which indicated a considerable departure from what we
called official accounts of the job. We now return to consider the implications of this for a marxist analysis. The
probation service's functions in support of capitalism are
not carried out smoothly and without interruption, nor are
structural constraints accepted without resistance. Although working-class struggle rarely directly affects the
probation service, there is a form of primitive resistance
from both probation officers and clients which is worth
examining.

We have cited many examples of probation officers' resistance in Part I. Back-region accounts of the work reveal that
social enquiry reports are often used directly to plead
leniency rather than to strive for objectivity; a blind eye may
be turned to failure to keep appointments rather than discipline being enforced; a reluctance to get work may be
accepted rather than breach action resulting. The coercive
mechanisms tend to be instigated as a last resort, if at all.
The guidelines for cash grants may be manipulated to meet

a particular need that is not covered. [17] Within the structural limitations imposed on them many probation officers try to organize their work with clients so as to maximize the benefits available and minimize the negative aspects, to make their work acceptable to their clients and to their own consciences. Such strategies are defended by reference to the need for discretion and professional autonomy in handling cases. Much of this resistance is on an individual basis but, increasingly, probation officers are prepared collectively to adopt a more oppositional stance to aspects of the juridical system through NAPO.

Clients, too, energetically resist the probation service's official purposes and this shows itself in many forms. Some appreciate the material help available, particularly in the form of cash, but have no use for the lengthy discussions of personal problems they are expected to endure. Others seek help with employment but show no interest in the value of work as a discipline and instead insist on a minimum acceptable wage as the first priority. Some clients are quite willing to go pony-trekking in Wales but sturdily resist the deeper significance of such worthwhile leisure pursuits and combine the outing with a heavy session in the local pub. Prisoners will cooperate willingly with their after-care officer in the hope of securing parole but following release are content to keep interviews brief and superficial. While social enquiry reports are being prepared, some clients express a keen interest in probation but after their court appearance fade out of sight and need to be cajoled to keep appointments. Some clients keep just enough contact to avoid breach action but render any planned programme of intervention redundant. Clients often refuse to accept the probation officer's definition of their needs and frustrate attempts to initiate discussion or action of which they disapprove. Probation officers can find such attitudes in their clients dispiriting and annoying but their significance should not be discounted. Nor should they, as they often are, be taken as personal failures or rejections; they are often accompanied by the client's perception of the probation officer as an acceptable individual.

We can draw some parallels between this kind of client resistance and that revealed in Paul Corrigan's study of working-class boys' attitudes to school. He describes their truancy, missing of particular lessons, adoption of a defiant pose and 'mucking about' in class as 'something to do with the boys' protection of themselves from things they don't like'.[18] He suggests that such activities are a primitive kind of 'fighting back'. The client resistance we have identified can be understood in the same way. For many clients the experience of the probation service is appreciated as an imposition, connected to their general experience of the law, the police, the courts and the prison. The probation officer is seen as upholding certain values – being in work, behaving yourself, keeping out of trouble, staying off the streets and doing something useful. The client reactions we have described represent a healthy refusal to accept these state definitions and parallel probation officers' own resistance to the structural role of the service.

THE PROBATION SERVICE – A MARXIST ANALYSIS

To draw together and summarize our analysis schematically we conclude that the probation service:

(1) *Is Part of the State Apparatus* which, like other parts:
– operates generally in the interest of capital
– has a degree of independence from the direct play of class interest
– has a 'surface appearance' of fuller independence – professionalism – which belies its true functions
– reflects in its operation such features of 'state form' as hierarchy and bureaucracy
– works through a combination of coercion and consent to secure the appearance of consensus in society.

(2) *Is Part of the State's Juridical System* which is the repository of the state's powers of coercion and like other parts of that system:
– preserves and promotes capitalist property relations and

important rules of behaviour
- assumes the 'fetishized form' of 'universality' through claims of scientific objectivity
- performs an important ideological role in securing and maintaining consent
- seeks to transform the offender into the obedient citizen under capitalism
- reacts to a 'crisis in hegemony' by moving to more coercive measures in the state's 'coercive tilt'.

(3) *Within the Juridical System has the Role* of:
- acting as the 'welfare arm' of the coercive apparatus
- undertaking the transformation of the offender without segregation and through obligation and cooperation secured by the exercise of mercy and discretion
- reproducing capitalist social relations by encouraging conformity, work, acceptance of authority, constructive leisure and maintenance of sex roles
- using the various methods of personal social work, backed by powers of coercion, to individualize and integrate offenders
- through this individualized, integrative work acting as a securer of consent for the penal system and, more generally, by promoting the image of a caring, consensus society.

We ended by pointing out that, despite this analysis and the problems it entails, the probation service's role and function are resisted by both probation officers and clients. The probation service is now, and will continue to be, an arena of struggle. In a real sense probation officers find themselves 'in and against the state'. In our final two chapters we will deal with the implications of this analysis for the struggles of practising probation officers and work towards some guidelines for practice.

PART III SOCIALIST PRACTICE

8
Towards Understanding

In this section we turn from the level of theory and analysis to the more practical and immediate level of day-to-day probation work, addressing the question, 'But what can we do in the job?' The inadequacies of previous attempts at prescriptions for radical practice warn us that the traps are legion. Some attempts seem to suggest that distinct 'radical social work practice and methods' exist which can resolve all the difficulties faced in the job, whilst others are so abstract and unrelated to everyday experience that they mean little to practitioners. Some prescriptions suggest that the brave individual can triumph, whilst others rest on a deterministic structural analysis and so argue that little can be achieved. Most prescriptions have little connection with analysis so that the contradictions, dilemmas and limitations of proposed strategies are not acknowledged. Many writers have, for example, unreservedly advocated working through the union without discussing the limits of that approach. Others have stressed the value of alliances without acknowledging the danger of incorporation. The failure to relate prescriptions to analysis has tended to lead to neglect of the connections between the state, the agency, the task and the method.

We have attempted to draw prescriptions from our analysis. We do not see the development of a distinct 'radical probation work' as a realistic aim, instead we emphasize the importance of a clear understanding of the issues faced in practice as the basis for determining appropriate action. In this first chapter we spell out what we see as the implications of our analysis and present a framework to aid understanding. In the next chapter we proceed to identify ways in which that understanding can be carried into action. Here we need to examine more closely the significance of our analysis for probation practice within the state. We look first at the structural limitations encountered and then discuss some fundamental contradictions which probation officers experience in their work. We then consider the relationship between the interests of probation clients and the general interests of the working class. Having looked at these various constraints, we consider the potential for socialist action in the probation service.

LIMITATIONS

A fundamental conclusion of our analysis is that probation officers are paid to do a particular job for the state and that this role is generally supportive of capitalism. Many people join the probation service in a conscious effort to escape from 'the rat race' of industry and commerce and may find this conclusion depressing. It is likely, however, to connect with their actual experience of the job and may help to make sense of the confusion encountered. This position of state employee limits the oppositional action possible in the job. There is room for manoeuvre and the limits are often unclear but some actions may simply be unacceptable. For example, clear statements of opposition to particular laws in social enquiry reports or open membership of PROP by a prison welfare officer may lead to some disciplinary action. Some projects and teams which have experimented with alternative ways of working or challenged conventions have, unwittingly, discovered that they were testing the permissible limits and have been closed down or dispersed.

As a consequence of their role, socialist probation officers will often find themselves at odds with their agency and should not expect to enlist official support. We need to be guarded about management supervision and cautious of agency initiatives and promises. Although sometimes we will be in agreement with the agency, and such alliances can be useful, they are likely to be short term and limited. Many aspects of the job, such as the conditions in probation orders and parole licences, are 'structured in'. These act as a constraint which tends to define the nature of contact with clients and may restrict flexibility in ways of working.

Our analysis clearly shows that some aspects of probation work which socialists will want to oppose are not obscure anomalies peculiar to the probation service, but fundamental features of the capitalist state and therefore will prove extremely resistant to challenge. Hierarchy, bureaucracy and individualization are examples of such state forms. Probation officers, for instance, recognize individualization in social enquiry reports as a focus for struggle because it ignores the communality of problems and isolates clients as pathological individuals. However, individualization is a basic feature of the whole of the capitalist criminal justice system and cannot be surmounted by an alternative social enquiry report practice. It will be right to pose challenges on such issues – this should not be done with a naive expectation of easy success but rather in full recognition of the significance of such struggles. We have argued that just being a probation officer involves upholding values and representing attitudes with which you may personally disagree. The role means that probation officers necessarily 'advertise' this capitalist ideology. Clients tend to assume that we stand for the value of work, the rule of law and the importance of deference to authority. Attempts to put forward alternative messages or to discuss difficulties realistically may not therefore be clearly perceived. This position of authority over clients is likely to affect our ability to influence them – in whatever direction! Efforts by probation officers to discuss issues with clients in a progressive way, for example by tackling sexist or racist attitudes, may encounter this obstacle. Clients may be reluctant to be involved in honest debate, particularly if the argument is likely to become heated. It is realistic to expect clients to be cautious in such situations – they have to watch their backs because we have significant powers over their lives. It is important to acknowledge the limitations which may arise from our relative position of authority.

In some public services guidelines for socialist action can be formulated by envisaging the form the service would take in a socialist society. For example in the fields of health care, education and housing such pre-figurative visions can guide the direction of struggle and act as an inspiration for positive change.[1] The analysis we have presented does not offer a similar vision for a socialist criminal justice system. There is disagreement among socialists about the role (if any) of prisons under socialism and we find it difficult to picture the probation service (if any) under socialism. This uncertainty means that there are no clear reference points to work towards. Another particular difficulty in the criminal justice field is that possibilities for alliances with other workers in related jobs are limited. Workers such as the police and prison officers carry out a more coercive function on behalf of the state and this affects their general orientation, making them unlikely allies.

It is important to bear in mind the relatively weak position of the probation service within the powerful criminal justice system and the coercive base of that system. This marginal status means that the probation service is rarely in a position to initiate change but rather follows developments in the criminal justice system. In a tilt towards coercion it is even conceivable that the consent-securing role of probation work might become redundant. Current shifts in the direction of a more coercive criminal justice system have instead produced pressures for authoritarian developments in the probation service. In understanding any such changes, probation officers must recognize and examine connections with the wider context of the state. In a coercive tilt opportunities for positive innovation will be limited but a defensive, oppositional stance is of great importance.

Having outlined these limitations, we argue that nevertheless there is considerable scope for struggle and socialist action within the role of probation officer, though it can never be a simple and straightforward job. However, it is possible that the sort of changes outlined above could so change the probation role that negatives predominate and opportunities for useful work and opposition become so limited that the job becomes unacceptable. For example projects, orders or licences which included extreme measures of control over the client might involve socialist probation officers in activity they find unjustifiable. Such a development is already foreshadowed by the Kent Probation Service's introduction of a 'Close Support Unit' and a 'Probation Control Unit'. Examples of controls introduced by these projects include:

> At 8.30 p.m. the trainees will leave the centre and will make their way home. Unit staff will be available until 10 p.m. to carry out spot checks to ensure that trainees arrive home within a reasonable time.[2]

> Under no circumstances are probationers permitted to respond to appointments offered by government departments, solicitors, etc. without first receiving permission from the Unit Probation Officer.[3]

> There is an expectation that probationers will respond immediately to any lawfully given instruction and the necessity to give any instruction more than twice should be considered as an infringement of the Unit's discipline code.[4]

There will be strenuous resistance from within the probation service to attempts to generalize such an approach.

CONTRADICTIONS

Our analysis suggests that there can be no absolute solutions or clear ways ahead in the job. All the possibilities and opportunities for socialist probation officers will also contain problems and dilemmas. We suggest that the marxist concept of the contradiction is helpful to understanding here. Contradictions stem from basic features of the capitalist system and cannot be resolved without fundamental change. As we grapple with issues in our work we uncover these contradictions which recur as problems and dilemmas. Identifying such contradictions helps to make sense of the confusion we face.

A primary contradiction arises because we work within definitions, with which we disagree, imposed by powerful institutions of the state. For example, working with laws we consider unjust and prisons we abhor places us immediately in a difficult and contradictory position. Such definitions cannot be escaped and we need to decide whether we can work positively despite them, living with the discomfort arising from this position. It may be helpful to be able to recognize the source of this discomfort.

Another major contradiction faced is that the aspects of the job which give both clients and probation officers room to manoeuvre – flexibility, discretion, autonomy and the brief to help – also produce other consequences. The exercise of discretion and mercy serves to legitimate the criminal justice system. The humane, welfare aspects of probation work represent a cost to the capitalist state but are also functional in securing consent. Another contradiction arises from the flexibility in the job which gives socialists the opportunity to work in humane and less oppressive ways. Equally it allows others to work in more authoritarian ways, for example by readily breaching or recommending recall. This use of flexibility can result in a lack of uniformity in dealings with clients – and thus potential injustices. For instance, how often clients are required to report will depend on the orientation of their probation officers. In other circumstances we might oppose the possibility of such inequity of treatment but attempts at standardization may well produce a more oppressive system.

Our analysis suggests that contradictions will also arise in day-to-day contact with clients. First, clients will tend to see us as authority figures and therefore keep some distance and censor their comments, despite our wish to encourage an open relationship and to 'get alongside' them. Second, our analysis identifies crime as a social and political construct which is unlikely to respond to individual attention. Thus probation work seems unable to attain the goal of helping individuals stay out of trouble. We will be disappointed that, irrespective of our efforts, clients often end up back in court. Third, there are contradictions related to providing material benefits for clients. The benefits we can obtain will usually be delivered in the state form and therefore be reinforcing capitalist social relations. Often they will prove woefully inadequate and so cannot be a fully satisfactory solution. Helping clients with practical problems in this way poses the familiar contradiction that such individual assistance ignores the communality of problems and cannot attack the source of need.

CRIME AND THE WORKING CLASS

We now turn to an area which has rarely been given attention in the radical literature but which we consider an important issue for socialist probation officers to explore, that is the relationship between our work with clients, crime and the working class. In our analysis we looked briefly at working-class experience of the law and now examine some of the issues arising from our perspective and its implications for practice. This is a preliminary and exploratory discussion which requires further attention.

We have noted that the probation service deals mainly with working-class clients, as a direct result of the way in which the law demarcates certain forms of activity as illegal. Working-class experience and attitudes towards crime are contradictory. Working people are concerned about crime and threats to their safety and property posed by offenders. Their experience of the damage and hurt caused by criminal activity is often real (although the extent to which people's lives are directly affected by crime remains unclear). However, their fears are fed by the media's sensational reporting of, and intense concentration on, crime and by the way in which the state consistently presents it as a major problem faced by working people. This misleading representation, together with the false 'fetishized' form of the law, leads working people to believe that the law can and will offer them the protection they need. So calls for 'law and order' can attract substantial working-class support. At the same time, this surface appearance of neutrality is often penetrated. Working people recognize that the law and its enforcement are not impartial and bear down disproportionately on them. Frequently they recognize that some of those labelled as criminal are not an alien threat but ordinary people much like themselves. Support for harsh punishment of 'criminals' can contrast sharply with a tolerant and sympathetic concern for offenders personally known.

We have noted that 'moral panics' around crime are used as a rationale for the strong state. Governments of whichever political hue seek to prove their suitability to govern by their ability to deal with crime, uniformly presented as a serious threat to society. Thus in most respects there is little distinction to be drawn between the penal policies of the main political parties – the Labour Party, the traditional party of the working class, displays the contradictory attitudes we have described. Not surprisingly there have been few working-class struggles in the area of crime and the law. The major exception to this occurs when traditional trade union rights and activities are criminalized or are threatened with criminalization, as with the opposition to the Industrial Relations Act 1971 or current resistance to changes in picketing law. Even when this happens, the connections between such 'political' crime and other crime are not made. The law is rarely dealt with as an issue for working-class struggle in politics. A recent exception to this has been the 'Sus' campaign, which succeeded in enlisting support from the labour movement.

Probation officers' orientation in their work and focus of concern has traditionally been almost exclusively with the offender. This has often been taken to the extreme of unreservedly championing the interests of the client and ignoring the impact of offences and the damage sometimes resulting for other working people. These attitudes arise from humane concern for the client, reinforced by the role specification (the brief to be concerned) and the social work emphasis of the job. There are dangers in this orientation because a total concern for the client is held at the expense of a more balanced approach, acknowledging the realities and problems of crime. It is consistent with our analysis to adopt a more even-handed approach. This would involve a shift away from the position of unqualified support for clients towards a more rounded concern with crime in so far as it is a problem for the working class. We need, however, to keep crime in perspective as a problem. It is by no means the greatest threat faced by the working class and we should refute that view by counterposing the greater threats – exploitation, low wages, injustice and inadequate welfare services.

POTENTIAL

We have dealt with the limitations and contradictions experienced in probation work in some detail because we consider that they have often been treated unrealistically in other radical prescriptions for practice. However, we do not see these constraints as disabling and believe there remains considerable scope for useful and progressive work by socialists within the probation service. Here we present a broad outline of this potential, which we develop in terms of concrete action in the final chapter.

It is helpful to retain a sense of perspective about the difficulties socialist probation officers encounter, because they work in service of a capitalist system. All socialist workers face similar limitations and contradictions in their work. Teachers, for instance, find themselves educating kids for exploitation or unemployment and efforts to approximate to a socialist approach to education encounter formidable institutional obstacles. Some workers find themselves in extremely hostile situations. Print workers speak of working in 'the Fleet Street lie factory' – imagine helping to produce the *Daily Telegraph* or *Daily Mail*! Workers in manufacturing and basic industries are seen as the key to socialist struggle but their daily work produces the profits which fuel the capitalist system. Short of stopping work, they have little opportunity to introduce their socialism to their day-to-day work. The Lucas Aerospace Shop Stewards Combine Committee provides a rare but encouraging example of positive socialist proposals emerging from adverse circumstances. Here a group of workers engaged in producing weaponry drew up alternative plans for using existing skills and machinery to manufacture socially useful products.[5] Probation officers opting out of the 'rat race' may not have escaped the system but they have found a job providing considerable room for manoeuvre in which it is worthwhile trying to develop a socialist practice.

By facing some of the difficulties involved in probation work and identifying some limitations, socialists open themselves to the criticism that their approach is negative. Our assessment of the positive potential of probation work may contrast unfavourably with many schemes that students and others will have encountered. We think that many conventional accounts of probation and social work are hopelessly ambitious, overstating the potential of social work for transforming both individuals and society. To present a more realistic base of expectation may seem an anti-climax but it is likely to equip people better to face the difficulties of practice.

Much existing social work theory rests on a fairly uncritical attitude to the society in which practice is located. The work of social workers can then be portrayed as positive action assisting the client to accommodate constructively within a beneficent society. Radical social work literature starts from a different evaluation of society and this inevitably affects what action can be viewed as positive. In our view, a continuing emphasis on the search for positive and initiating strategies has led to an undervaluing of the importance of defensive and oppositional action. Socialist probation officers find themselves working within a criminal justice system, much of which they oppose. Whatever the scope for other action, they will find themselves seeking to protect people from the worst consequences of the system, resisting its values and opposing the way it works. In *The Politics of Abolition,* Thomas Mathieson points out the importance of negating action which works for the 'abolition of whatever gave or gives legitimacy of a system you regard as wrong. Thereby you *unmask* the attempts of the system to mask its true nature: you *unveil* whatever the system veils'.[6] Socialist probation officers must be alert to the fact that injunctions to 'think positive' or to 'think constructively' can often simply mean 'start thinking like us' and are invitations to abandon their political perspective. Here we wish to stress the positive nature of opposition within an antagonistic criminal justice system. In a period of coercive tilt, an oppositional stance will be particularly important: changes in the job will need to be resisted and the opportunities for progressive development are likely to be limited.

We have argued that the juridical system plays a crucial role in legitimizing the capitalist state. This close inter-connectedness necessarily makes it a difficult area for struggle and leads to many limitations on possibilities for action. Equally though, the fact that the criminal justice system underpins the capitalist state makes it a vital arena for struggle. A major role of the juridical system lies in its ideological function. Resistance to this ideology from within the system is an important contribution to its 'unmasking' and 'unveiling'. It matters that there are *probation officers* prepared to state publicly that prison is destructive, that there are unjust laws, that law enforcement is discriminatory and even that the probation service cannot cope with the poverty and hardship our work uncovers. It could be even more effective if magistrates, police officers and prison staff were also prepared to dissent: their silence places even more responsibility on probation officers. The whole burden of opposition and exposure otherwise falls on those processed by the system, offenders whose credibility is easily undermined. Socialist probation officers, together with lawyers and others, are well placed to make this important contribution of exposing the role of the criminal justice system to critical debate.

Here we are identifying potential for probation officers to contribute to 'struggle within the state'. Although we have argued that such struggle alone will not lead to radical change within society, it is an important adjunct to struggle in the economic sphere. It can pose significant challenges to capitalist social relations, to the ideology of state institutions and to the nature of the state apparatus. As well as posing challenges within the criminal justice system probation officers gain knowledge and experience relevant to struggles in the welfare state. They can contribute to struggles being waged over housing, education and poverty. Again, what probation officers do and say gains significance from their position of employment within the state, and gains credibility because it is based on knowledge drawn from experience in the job.

Many radical prescriptions have emphasized the role of such campaigning without being very specific about how it can be done. We hope to give this some attention in the next chapter. Its importance needs emphasis because we are only too aware how easy it is to get bogged down in the immediate pressures of work with clients. Sometimes putting energy into taking a motion to your union branch or supplying information to a campaign seems a side issue. Or you may fully intend to do something about it later but put in on one side only for it to be overtaken by some new crisis. The stereotype of social workers who put all their energy into campaigning at the expense of their clients is a cheap and cruel caricature. The pressures of the job too often take people to the opposite extreme. Socialist probation officers must find time and use opportunities to take their knowledge and experience beyond individual probation practice.

It will remain the case that most of us spend most of our time in direct probation work with clients. This places a premium on developing a constructive and progressive practice consistent with a socialist analysis. The potential we have already identified also creates the basis for such practice. The welfare role of the probation service and the discretion and flexibility available contribute to creating 'space' for progressive work with clients. Clients can also benefit from our rejection of retrogressive attitudes and approaches. Realism about what might or might not be achieved with and for clients will be an improvement on visionary utopianism based on some ambitious social work theory. Defensive and oppositional action will also have an important place in individual practice. Social enquiry reports can seek to lessen the oppressive effect of the criminal justice system. In probation work we can seek to minimize the negative and repressive aspects of the job. The results of such action may not appear as a dramatic new practice, but they will be experienced and appreciated by clients. In personal practice too the positive nature of defensive action should not be underestimated.

Our perception and understanding of the state, the criminal justice system and issues in the welfare state can be brought into work with clients. This will affect both the way we view and talk about the difficulties facing them and the action taken in response to those difficulties. The 'space' available in the job also allows us to act humanely and with consideration towards clients, qualities rare in the criminal justice system. Opportunities exist to take account of and respect clients' views and attitudes. Finally we can use our position to provide and devise services which are genuinely useful and helpful to clients. Within the limitations and constraints we have outlined, the emphasis on autonomy of judgement and decision in the probation role provides considerable potential in which to develop a socialist practice.

FRAMEWORK FOR UNDERSTANDING

In this chapter we have sought in broad terms to evaluate the limitations and potential of probation work. In the final chapter we shall look at how these ideas can be translated into action. Before doing so, we need to re-emphasize our belief that an adequate understanding of the issues faced is the crucial basis of socialist probation practice. We are concerned to leave readers in a position to apply our analysis to a range of situations they will face in the job. We therefore conclude this chapter with an outline 'framework for understanding', which we hope will prove a useful analytical tool. We have set out some questions based on our general analysis which we suggest can be specifically applied to problems faced. In the questions the pronoun 'it' is used to mean the issue examined, whether it is a social work method, a policy proposal, a new project or one of the basic tasks of the service. Answering the questions will not provide a neat solution. Not every question will apply to a particular issue and the various factors will still need to be weighed against each other, but the framework may identify aspects which would otherwise have been neglected or undervalued.

The State

Placing a particular issue within the wider context of the role and function of the state under capitalism helps us to understand the often conflicting and contradictory aspects of the job, the relative significance of this aspect of probation work, how it connects with and contributes to the state's function. It helps to place the issue in a broader perspective and may identify relevant areas of struggle. So we suggest asking:

- What connections can be identified with the functions of the state?
- What values does it promote?
- Does it contribute to the securing of consent? To which part of the state apparatus and in what way?
- What other parts of the state apparatus are particularly relevant here? What role do they play? Do their definitions predominate? Does it support/strengthen/adopt/ oppose those definitions?
- Does it relate to changes within the state?
- What potentially oppositional features can be identified?
- What connections are there with struggles in the state?

Clients

Having located the issue within the structure of the state we need to assess its impact on clients. We need to identify what it will mean to them and what their response will be. So we suggest asking:

– What is the impact on clients and their families? Are benefits provided/won? If so, under what conditions and in what form?
– What restrictions does it impose?
– What messages and values does it convey to clients?
– How much real consent can clients exercise?
– What do clients say about it? What is their reaction?

The Working Class

Our understanding should extend to the impact on working people and consider connections with issues relevant to the working class as a whole. So we suggest asking:

– What impact will it have on the working class?
– Does it relate to problems faced by the working class as a whole?
– Can connections be made with working-class struggles?

The Probation Role

Finally, we need to appreciate the significance of issues for the way they affect our work and whether they involve changes in the role of probation officers.

– What are the main features of the role here with clients and with other state institutions?
– What does this role mean for the way probation officers work?
– What opportunities are there for individual discretion and autonomy?
– Does it imply a change in the probation role and in what direction?
– What are the major contradictions and dilemmas it involves?

9
Socialist Probation Practice

In presenting our prescriptions for socialist probation practice we cannot go beyond establishing broad guidelines which people can then apply intelligently to their day-to-day work. Wherever possible we include examples to clarify our proposals. We will present our prescriptions divided into three main spheres of activity – personal practice, the agency and the union – identifying the possibilities for progressive action in each. Our analysis makes it clear that decisions about the appropriate response to a particular issue will involve examining both limitations and potential before deciding on balance what approach to adopt. We therefore end by suggesting some questions to help clarify what action is appropriate in a particular situation, taking into account the problems faced.

PERSONAL PRACTICE

Many of the suggestions we make in this section will already instinctively form part of the practice of some probation officers. However, there is value in relating them coherently to a firm analysis. We have rejected the search for 'the radical method' and instead suggest that a more fruitful way ahead is to concentrate on approach and orientation. It is more useful to aim for clarity about the possibilities and limitations of the job, to look for ways of exploiting potential and minimizing negatives.

Our overarching theme will be that understanding should permeate all aspects of the job. Thus our socialist perspective should affect our approach to clients, our appreciation of their problems, our attitude to solutions to those problems and the way in which we tackle the various bits of the job. This involves resisting the correctionalist perspective underpinning much probation work. We identify three main approaches consequent on this orientation. First, resisting the communication of capitalist ideology and social relations in the job and where possible using opportunities to present an oppositional viewpoint. To illustrate we give an example of each:

Faced with unemployed clients, don't end up nagging them about work. Be realistic about local employment prospects and offer help only if they want it. Respect their views about a decent living wage and don't press them to accept low-paid jobs. Don't try to persuade them that work ennobles the spirit.

You will often find yourself talking about women with young male clients, particularly about their girlfriends and mothers. This will present opportunities to gently tackle sexist stereotypes, question their attitudes and move towards presenting alternative views of the role of women.

Second, there are opportunities to expose and resist state forms, while recognizing their strength and significance. When working with clients on problems over DHSS and housing, chances arise for general discussion about why the system is obstructive and difficult. We can relate their experience to a wider political perspective without imposing our views. The job provides plenty of scope to discuss the true nature of the criminal justice system with offenders who have been processed by it. Clients often freely voice their feelings about this and such occasions can be used to relate personal experiences to a more political perspective. We need to identify practices which resist the state form:

Although individualization is a basic feature of the legal system, we can work against it in our practice with clients. Don't become obsessed with individual pathology but instead recognize and emphasize similarities with other people. Let clients see clearly that the criminal justice system seeks to 'split them off' but that your approach is different.

Third, we should adopt an open and honest approach with clients so they can be clear about our role and relationship with them. Clients should be aware of the constraints operating on us – that we are supervised and accountable – and the implications of this for them. They need to know that written records may be subject to inspection and that reports prepared on them may have wider distribution and be forwarded to a prison or hostel. They need to know the possible dangers which might arise from total honesty. Implicit in this open approach is being clear with clients about the unequal nature of our relationship with them:

The idea of 'contracts' may be popular with your colleagues and in your agency. However, the surface appearance of equality in 'contracts' masks the unequal relationship between clients and probation officers. Clarity includes recognition of the power relationship between you and your clients.

Within this overall approach we now turn to examine six areas of progressive practice.

Defensive Work

We have already commented on the positive nature of opposition within an antagonistic system and suggest that in personal practice this mostly takes the form of seeking to defend clients against the worst features of the capitalist state. One main concern will be defending clients against the criminal justice system. To some extent we can influence decisions about offenders' liberty through social enquiry, home circumstances and parole reports, seeking to minimize the use of custody:

Progressive social enquiry report practice includes the following features. Being prepared to stress positives in clients' circumstances and to create positives where necessary by, for instance, arranging accommodation for the homeless in custody. Never recommending immediate or suspended custodial sentences, wherever possible being ready with an alternative recommendation.

A similar defence against the structures of the job will be necessary. We should make minimum use of breach and recall procedures and resist the insertion of additional specific conditions within orders. This defensive approach will also be appropriate in connection with other parts of the state apparatus – for instance, arguing for delay in eviction or disconnection of fuel supply in the hope of creating opportunities to prevent such action.

Helping

It follows from our analysis of the criminal justice and social systems as harsh and oppressive to the working class that probation work will bring you into contact with people who have considerable material and emotional needs. We suggest that efforts to ease the way for clients constitute a small-scale attempt to redress the balance. We define 'helping' work as actions which clients consider useful to them. Bottoms and McWilliams have advocated the substitution of 'client-defined help' for treatment in probation practice, and we welcome this orientation.[1] However, we find their concept of 'unconditional help' unrealistic. It is important to acknowledge constraints; probation officers cannot always meet requests made by clients, and similarly clients will be limited in the kind of help they can ask of probation officers. Given this qualification, however, we think that probation officers should be willing to help clients in the ways they request. This will involve both practical and emotional help, and first we consider practical help.

Many problems experienced by clients clearly require financial assistance but the probation service has traditionally exhibited a confused attitude to giving out money. The need is recognized in that all services make some provision by way of befriending and other funds. Yet the attitude to making grants is parsimonious, and the amounts allowed are often too small to meet needs realistically or too hedged about with conditions to be useful. We think that a socialist practice requires a much more straightforward approach. We should be unambiguously prepared to consider, and where possible meet, clients' requests for financial help. Where funds are inadequate we should pressurize for better provision within the agency and for procedures to be simplified. As part of an introduction to the services available, clients should be informed of the availability of cash grants. A similar attitude is required to other forms of material aid in kind. We are not suggesting that this should take the place of demands on other agencies or that the probation service should take over responsibility for primary provision, but that we need to identify unmet or inadequately met needs and act on them.

Other sorts of practical help can be offered. This could mean active support, guidance and advice for those in difficulties with housing, the DHSS and gas or electricity boards. It might mean encouraging clients to use the facilities and resources of the office – for instance, to make important phone calls or get a letter typed or photocopied. This concept of the probation office as a facility for clients offers considerable scope for development and innovation. Sometimes clients will want to be accompanied to Supplementary Benefit offices or Job Centres, or to be represented at a tribunal. Occasionally the best way of helping a client will be providing transport.

One problem immediately posed by this commitment to helping is the pressure placed on our time and the difficulty in determining priorities between competing demands. We need to consider whether the help of others can be enlisted in these tasks. It is important to be clear about what can and cannot be achieved, about what it is sensible to attempt. Wild promises of help that we are unable to keep are misleading and unfair. Attention also needs to be given to the form in which any help given is delivered. We should try to avoid putting clients in embarrassing or demeaning positions because of their need to accept assistance from the probation service.

The place of emotional help in probation work has tradi-tionally been given an extremely high priority and its importance has been overstated. Many clients of the pro-bation service do not seek or require such help. Where, however, clients clearly need and desire emotional help, probation officers should be prepared to endeavour to relieve distress. Often the needs that are presented do not require a complex, therapeutic approach and sympathetic counselling will suffice. Probation officers deal with some relatively isolated people and the needs they bring are those that would otherwise be met through everyday contact with friends or relatives. Where long-term support will be necessary, care has to be taken not to foster unrealistic expectations and consideration should be given to other means of meeting such needs.

We have criticized conventional methods of approaching emotional problems, highlighting the dangers and limita-tions of focusing on individual pathology and failing to consider social and political factors. We must avoid urging acceptance on clients distressed because of material and practical problems. This can weaken resistance to injus-tices, bad housing or poverty and suggest that anger or depression are not legitimate responses to such conditions. It may be equally irresponsible to suggest resistance as a solution in certain situations – for instance to a prisoner having to cope with the pressures of the institution. Pro-bation officers constantly face conflicts arising from the relationship between individual distress and structural issues. Recently there have been attempts to reconcile the apparently disparate spheres of the personal and the political. This has not been our primary concern and readers will need to turn to other writings to pursue the theme. We believe the women's movement in particular has recog-nized the importance of making these connections and has worked towards the development of non-oppressive forms of therapy.[2]

Educational Work

Some writers have stressed the educative function of social work but we think it important to stress that education is a two-way process. There are things which clients can usefully learn from us but we must also be prepared to learn from clients. They have direct experience, for instance, of social security, the police and prisons, which we may lack. It is important to value their accounts and learn from them if our advice is to be useful to others. In attempts to help clients with problems we should always be prepared to share any knowledge which we have and which may be useful to them. An effort should be made to equip clients with the skills they may need to tackle similar problems in the future. Wherever possible, knowledge and skills should be passed on in such a way that they can be applied to a variety of situations, so that learning can be generalized:

Some clients have difficulty in keeping the electricity board, for example, at bay. Having poor standards of literacy and being too embarrassed to make part payment at the showroom, they ignore bills until disconnection is inevitable. A model letter can be drafted which they can copy and send off with part payment and promise of instalments. The letter, and the technique, can act as a model for similar responses to other debts.

We will need to look for knowledge and skills which clients don't have but could use, and which they consider would be worth acquiring. Many clients will have had bad experiences of the state education system and it will be important to find styles of educational work which avoid the patronizing and hierarchical features of the state form.

Developing Useful Services

An important criterion for action should be the test of usefulness to clients. Where we identify needs, we should work to develop services which start to meet them. Often it will be wasteful or impossible to provide services to individuals and then we should concentrate on needs common to a number of clients. Sometimes it will be possible to do this within personal practice but more often it involves pressing for services to be established within the agency. Examples of some such existing services are good-quality bedsit accommodation provision, social clubs for isolated clients and bus services for visitors to remote prisons.

The same criterion of usefulness can be used to evaluate social work methods and projects. We have made it clear that new methods and new projects are not our answer to the question of what is progressive practice. However, they may have a part to play in providing flexibility and a range of useful services to clients. Each proposal has to be examined on its merits and its limitations and potential weighed up before deciding whether it deserves support. Sometimes methods or projects can be modified to increase their usefulness and diminish their correctional content as in the following examples:

It is proposed in your office that a group work approach should be adopted with unsupported mothers and their children. You are interested and go along to a planning session. You are horrified to hear the ideas that others have – teaching 'good mothering', homecraft and other useful womanly skills! However, you are able to point out to colleagues the values they are promoting and persuade them to focus the group more on the provision of a crèche, self-help activities and some consciousness-raising discussion.

Your service has succeeded in securing funds from an oil company to establish a bike project for young adults, involving evening garage work and weekend scrambling. You support in principle the provision of such a useful leisure service in the area. However, it is proposed that it be available only to those attending as a condition of their probation order. Sentenced to pleasure! You are determined to resist such a restriction and mobilize colleagues to threaten a dearth of referrals. Equally, you resist compromise talk of 'contracts' of commitment to the scheme. When eventually the scheme starts, the clients are eager to participate voluntarily and you manage to persuade the organizers to accept 'mates' who are not clients of the service.

Community Involvement

A fairly coherent critique of community work has emerged from the literature of radical social work but this has little application to the probation service, where community involvement remains largely an unexplored area. There are obstacles arising from the probation service's relative isolation from the local community – typically an office caseload involves contact with only a tiny proportion of homes in the area. Too often community involvement means little more than getting to know the other agencies in the area, attending social workers' lunches where 'ganging up on clients' flourishes. There is evidence of a more elaborated approach emerging – Bottoms and McWilliams advocate a form of community involvement by the probation service which they describe as 'micro-structural amelioration'.[3] This poses several problems, perhaps most seriously that its primary aim of 'crime reduction' lays it open to worrying correctionalist interpretations. At a recent conference a probation team adopting Bottoms and McWilliams's 'paradigm' had developed a style of community involvement which to us seemed closer to 'community surveillance'.[4] This relates to other recent developments in combating delinquency and truancy through inter-agency cooperation involving schools, social services departments, probation services and police forces, which introduce new dimensions of surveillance – all under the harmless label of 'community programmes'.[5]

Despite these difficulties community involvement presents important opportunities for progressive practice. Good community links and knowledge of what is going on locally are necessary if we are to help clients effectively. Practice based on wanting to do everything yourself is inappropriate – if we are to use other sources of support and pressure groups, encouraging clients to seek collective solutions, then we have to make contacts which make introductions easy. Community involvement could be used to demonstrate that offenders' problems are common to the community and has potential for developing a dialogue at a local level concerning working-class experience of, and concern about, crime. It also provides one channel for carrying forward oppositional stances. We have experience and ability which can be useful to local groups. In the job we accumulate information and knowledge which can be of assistance, as well as having access to resources, facilities and sources of information which can be tapped. Involvement with, for instance, local Cuts Campaigns, the Trades Council, tenants' organizations and claimants' unions, enables us to broaden our ability to 'struggle within the state' and to take criminal justice issues into the working-class movement.

Campaigning Action

We have advocated a helping approach in personal practice but clearly acknowledge the limitations of 'patching-up' action in which the source of problems is not tackled. In our discussion of potential in the last chapter we stressed the importance of campaigning action and said we would give this some attention here. It is often suggested that social workers should supplement 'patching-up' help with action through the union and other organizations aimed at tackling the causes of social problems. It is clearly unrealistic to suggest that the individual probation officer can launch, or work in, campaigns on each of the myriad of issues which arise in the job. We need to act selectively in terms of actual involvement and on most issues our role will be to supply others with information and experience. Even this is easier said than done – in practice it requires considerable discipline and the machinery for the routine collection and use of such information will usually not exist. But development of this sort of involvement in campaigning would be a positive and realistic step forward for probation officers.

Sometimes campaigning action will appropriately be carried out through the union, and we return to this later, but it will also be important to contribute to other campaigning organizations and pressure groups. Such work will not come easily to many probation officers and requires them to learn different skills from those in which they are trained. To be useful, information needs to be presented clearly and in an easily assimilated form, for instance as case histories dramatically highlighting the issue of concern. Machinery needs to be established so that people find it easier to contribute information, knowing that it will be constructively used. More active involvement in selected campaigns requires further development of skills in writing, pamphleteering, public speaking and dealing with the media. Probation officers often feel very strongly about their experiences and need to explore new ways of bringing these issues to public attention.

In pursuing campaigning work we need to be aware of its limitations. Campaigns are inevitably seeking reforms and we have already noted the contradictory consequences of reform. Even when concessions are won they will be shaped according to ruling-class interests and rarely represent more than a partial gain. We have already mentioned the 'Sus' campaign as a rare example of effective mobilization in the area of law. Sadly it seems quite probable that the sus laws may be repealed, only to be replaced by a modern and more refined statute criminalizing the same activities. When limited reforms are achieved they frequently require continuing campaigns in their defence. The 1967 Abortion Act provides an outstanding example of this.[6] Campaigning groups face acute problems in orientation. Some pitch their demands so as to secure credibility with those in power and consequently risk incorporation. A more direct and radical approach may make more relevant demands but risks being defined out and ignored. Mick Ryan's analysis of the Howard League and Radical Alternatives to Prison illustrates this point in the field of penal reform.[7]

IN THE AGENCY

As in personal practice, work within the agency needs to reflect our understanding. One immediate consequence of this is that we need to anticipate that we will not be in complete harmony with the agency. Conflicts will arise from the agency's commitment to carry out its function in support of the capitalist state. A major source of tension will be the ways in which the organization of the probation service embodies the state form. Its hierarchical and bureaucratic structure is experienced as oppressive and limiting, often seeming perversely obstructive. It is tempting to blame the individual managers and radicals sometimes think promotion may be a way to change the agency – if they were making the decisions things would be different! Our analysis indicates that such a strategy is likely to prove extremely limited. The agency will be more resistant than the individual and a corrosive process of accommodation is inclined to set in.

It is particularly difficult to generalize about the potential for socialist action within the agency. What you are able to do will depend on what you have to cope with in your particular team, office and probation service. You need to strike a balance between your desire to put forward socialist ideas, discuss them with colleagues and challenge management, and your need to be comfortable at work, develop useful relationships and survive. We deal first with a discussion of the problems of survival before proceeding to identify four more positive areas of progressive practice.

Survival

How you decide to operate within your agency will ultimately have to be a personal decision based on local circumstances. You need to make tactical decisions about what risks to take and at times will need to exercise some caution. For example, students and unconfirmed probation officers are in a particularly vulnerable position. Depending on their supervisor or senior, they may find their possibilities for socialist action restricted. Experienced probation officers may not be able to put their analysis into action without unduly exposing themselves to disciplinary action or dismissal. So we suggest that you should assess the potential in your own situation, weigh the risks and then decide what action is appropriate.

It is wise to guard against unnecessary criticism. Management scrutiny tends to concentrate on written records and the keeping of up-to-date minimal records is an important safeguard. Often work with clients will have to be justified in the sort of language management prefers – references to esoteric social work theories, the needs of the relationship and professional judgement will prove useful. If you are known to hold different ideas, others in your team and office may pay particular attention to the way you behave. Socialist probation officers should therefore act reliably towards colleagues, shouldering their share of the work and behaving with consideration, but setting realistic limits so as not to wear themselves out. Struggling on unable to do anything properly and making promises we cannot keep will do our cause no good.

For protection and sanity it is essential to seek out alliances. We need support in the work from people who can share frustrations and discuss ways forward, so we need to recognize dissatisfactions in our colleagues. Within the office or team limited alliances are usually possible on some issues. Sharing a problem with a colleague or working together on an issue may provide an opportunity to extend the area of agreement. Almost certainly it will be necessary to look outside the office to find others sharing a socialist perspective. The union will be one source of support but may tend to operate along rather formalized lines and so fail to provide sufficient scope for informal discussion. In some union branches ad hoc groups have been established around particular issues to meet this need. The NAPO Members' Action Group works through local groups which meet regularly and provide socialists with opportunities for mutual support, discussion of issues and joint action.

Defensive and Oppositional Work

We must emphasize the positive value of defensive work within the agency. By now our general meaning will be

clear and, in the particular context of the agency, energy
will be directed towards resisting the pressures and limitations which management seek to impose. We need to
defend the autonomy and space which permit progressive
practice and support the kinds of work which provide help
for clients in a non-oppressive way. Socialist probation
officers should monitor developments within the agency
and be prepared to resist shifts towards more repressive
measures. Watch for the form that new resources take and
be ready to oppose the channelling of staff and money into
projects which restrict clients' ability to choose. We
illustrate the kind of action we mean:

A leak from management meeting minutes indicates that plans
are afoot to tighten up on inspection of probation supervision
with a view to initiating more breaches in an effort to improve
credibility with the courts. You immediately consult colleagues
and find widespread support for opposing this clamp-down.
Together you arrange an emergency office meeting to discuss the
issue; the seniors are defensive and argue that the plan was only a
discussion document. They are concerned at the united resistance to increased scrutiny shown; even the right wing in the
office consider it a diminution of their professional authority. The
seniors agree to oppose the idea at the next management
meeting; it is decided to raise the issue at the next local NAPO
meeting and also to gather ammunition for the argument – the
last four breaches to be heard in court led to continuation of the
orders; the proportion of probation orders in the office caseload is
high, so where is the loss of credibility?

Developing Useful Services

In dealing with this in the section on personal practice we
indicated that usually useful services would need to be
developed on an agency basis. The agency should be
pressed to devote resources to the provision of services
which clients define as useful. Where the service is initiating projects we can make efforts to deflect them from a
correctional orientation and towards a 'service' approach.
To a limited extent it may also be possible to enlist agency

support for useful services based outside the probation service.

Educational Work

There will be many opportunities within the agency to pose alternative points of view, challenge conventional thinking and present socialist ideas in a well-argued and relevant way. We should make use of chances to spread progressive practice to both colleagues and students. Apart from formal educational opportunities, such as in-service training, study days and courses, we can use both routine team meetings and informal discussions to present arguments. Educational work should not be confined to discussion and argument – we should be prepared to set an example by the way we behave. For instance, the way we treat secretaries can demonstrate non-sexist attitudes and our general response to clients can act as an example of humanity and consideration. Finally we can also influence the type of education that takes place within the agency by requesting progressive books for the office library and pressing for alternative speakers on in-service training courses. We should also take opportunities to be involved in supervising students and to participate in local training courses.

Collective Work

In principle socialists should aim to work cooperatively and collectively as this is one way of countering individualization. The opportunities for such work will depend upon the particular situation in your team, office and service. Where collective work is possible it will have many advantages. The problems which clients share emerge more clearly and communal solutions can be pursued. This can also encourage a better use of information gained in the job and might lead to its use in campaigning. Team decision-making should be encouraged because this acts as a counter to the hierarchical state form and offers a practical example of alternative forms of organization. Collective working also helps to counter the individualization of the probation officer by, for example, reducing the impact of management supervision on the individual's confidence. Working co-operatively encourages the sharing of problems, helps to develop common understanding and promotes positive approaches to the job. We give a simple example:

Team discussion and allocation of new cases removes sole control of information from the senior and allows it to be shared amongst team members. This knowledge of the team's intake allows common problems to be identified and sentencing patterns to be monitored. Talking over new cases gives you the opportunity to influence colleagues' practice and makes it easier to suggest shared or group work approaches.

We recognize that some isolated socialists will have only limited opportunities for collective work and will have to give priority to creating space for their own individual progressive practice. It is important to recognize that our proposals are limited and may have other consequences. Managers have also seen the team approach as a productive one and identified the team as an effective channel for their views. Under their model the senior becomes management's representative in the office and the team responds to action-centred leadership rather than developing a co-operative approach. Probation officers become isolated in their teams and consultation is carried out through line management, reducing the possibility of discussion, action and negotiation on a wider basis through the union. So, although we advocate collective action within the agency, we stress that probation officers need also to work through an organization that is not part of the management structure – the union.

THE UNION

For socialists the union is an essential arena for struggle. It is also a promising area of work for a number of reasons. It is relatively independent of management structures and pro-

bation service employers. It offers members the protection
of strength in numbers and the potential solidarity of
collective action, as well as defence in event of disciplinary
action. As an organization formed by the combination of (in
theory) equal members, it has considerable potential for
democracy and responsiveness. Finally, work in the union
allows connections to be made with other workers through
the trade union movement and with other working-class
organizations. The union for probation officers, NAPO, has a
high proportion of officers in membership and has un-
challenged negotiating rights for them. The union can act as
a vehicle for pursuing progressive policies and presenting
alternatives to state ideology. In some ways it acts as a
particular form of 'campaigning' organization. Its particular
strength is that it cannot readily be defined out because of
its inherent legitimacy and power of action. Socialists will
find potential for work both through the union – arguing for
progressive policies – and for the union – helping it to
function and carry out policy. The union may not, of
course, be a ready-made vehicle for progressive action and
considerable work may have to go into transforming it into
an effective and democratic organization. In this respect
NAPO provides a good example of what can be achieved and
most of its members recognize that over the past ten years it
has developed from a weak, conservative and manage-
ment-dominated professional association towards being an
active, representative and progressive trade union.

Some commentators have uncritically advocated work in
the union but it is important to recognize the limitations of
this strategy. Unions do not occupy a position entirely
autonomous from the state. They are partly incorporated
organizations which have been encouraged as a means of
dealing in an orderly way with dissent. Unions have
accommodated to the capitalist structure and are more used
to negotiating concessions than challenging its legitimacy.
In the process, unions are in danger of being influenced by
the values and ideology of capitalism, and of being con-
taminated by state forms of organization. There are further
weaknesses in a small union like NAPO, which can exercise

little economic muscle and is relatively powerless. NAPO also has a long way to go in terms of political development, evolving effective ways of pursuing policy and learning the value of solidarity. Despite these limitations there is considerable potential for socialist action within NAPO and we identify five main areas.

Oppositional Work

Throughout, we have stressed the positive value of defensive and oppositional work. The union is the main arena in which work can be done on the formulation and pursuit of oppositional policies. It is only through the union that policies can be pursued which express direct opposition to the more oppressive parts of the probation officer's job. This has proved a difficult area in which to make progress within NAPO because it impinges directly on probation officers' working lives. There have been proposals for abolition of statutory licences, including parole, and withdrawal from prison welfare work which have not been adopted. Some impact on NAPO policy has been made with a generalized opposition to suspended sentence supervision orders, support for a major review of the parole system and a lack of enthusiasm for statutory licences in response to recent policy proposals. The major success in this area has been NAPO's adoption of a policy of not preparing social enquiry reports in cases where the defendant is pleading not guilty:

Probation officers recognized their involvement as a potential injustice. They saw it as intrusive for an investigation to be conducted before a conviction, and feared that where a judge saw the report before a trial it might prejudice the defence or be used in plea bargaining. They resolved to oppose that by refusing to prepare such reports.

The union is also the main vehicle for opposing attempts to introduce more oppressive types of work. The major example was the Younger Report's proposals for two new orders giving probation officers additional powers in supervising young adult offenders,[8] which NAPO strongly opposed:

The Report advocated 'control in the community' with probation officers exercising wide controls and with limited but arbitrary powers of detention. Probation officers recognized and opposed this as a significant shift away from a social work orientation and towards correctionalism. NAPO effectively marshalled arguments against these proposals and contributed to their eventual abandonment.

The union provides probation officers with the opportunity to express opposition to features of the criminal justice system and to seek changes within it. A major focus here has been on oppressive laws and NAPO has supported the decriminalization of soliciting, sus and other vagrancy offences, drunkenness offences and possession of cannabis. NAPO is opposed to the excessive use of imprisonment and so has supported reductions in the powers of sentencers and the proposal to reduce maximum sentences. A recent policy concentrates on the position of remand prisoners:

Probation officers are concerned at the injustice of unconvicted prisoners spending long periods in custody awaiting trial. They supported a proposal (based on Scottish practice) that such remands should be limited to a maximum of 110 days. NAPO has promoted this policy through sympathetic MPs and it has been extensively discussed in recent parliamentary debates.

The union is also in a position to identify and oppose the encroaching, repressive activities of the state. NAPO has adopted policies of opposition to control units in the prison system, the introduction of tougher detention centre regimes and the practice of jury vetting. The union's oppositional stances need not be limited to the immediate work of the service and wider issues concerning the criminal justice system but can extend to a range of social policy matters. NAPO has, for instance, adopted oppositional policies in the fields of housing, immigration, cuts in public services and social security provision. These normally take the form of aligning NAPO with opposition from other unions and working-class movements.

In considering these five areas of oppositional work we have deliberately concentrated on issues which have already been discussed within NAPO or form part of the union's policy. There is considerable potential for further action along these lines.

Exposing Work

Within the union there is opportunity to pursue policies which draw attention to aspects of the state which it is functional for capital to keep masked, and thus expose its true nature. Such aspects include the coercive base of the state as revealed in prisons, the harsh nature of the penal system, the false appearance of the law and the fundamental inequalities that lie beneath formal 'justice' and 'rights'. The discussion of policy issues within the union presents many opportunities for such 'unveiling' and for relating particular issues to trends and shifts within the state. NAPO has adopted some oppositional policies which have a particular potential for this exposing work. NAPO has called for a public enquiry into the use of MUFTI squads and their deployment on 31 August 1979 in Wormwood Scrubs, and more generally for a repeal of the Official Secrets Act to remove the blanket of secrecy from prisons.

Promoting Progressive Practice

We have outlined proposals for progressive work in personal practice and within the agency. The union provides an opportunity, at local and national levels, to develop, promote and spread such practices. Within NAPO this function remains underdeveloped. It would be possible, for instance, for the union to organize a system for the collection and collation of probation officers' experiences and the use of this material in furthering relevant campaigns. NAPO has supported the development of welfare rights work and circulated advice to members concerning legislation on homelessness. NAPO's *Probation Journal* has considerable potential for publicizing progressive practice.

Educational Work

The union provides excellent opportunities for educational work. Because it operates through open debate other probation officers can be influenced and discussion is not limited to conventional wisdoms. Even in debating policies which are not particularly progressive, there are opportunities to introduce a socialist perspective. Influence can be exerted through proposing policies, taking part in debates at meetings, working on committees and contributing to publications. The attempt to translate policies into action highlights features of the capitalist state and so extends the educative process. The resources of the union also raise the possibility of providing alternative learning opportunities through the organization of short courses, conferences and sponsoring research. The union can also educate through working in ways which counter the state form and provide a prefigurative example of socialist styles of organization. The relative independence of the union allows the possibility of tackling sexism and racism, setting an example for action on a wider scale. Hierarchical and bureaucratic tendencies can be countered by insisting on a direct, responsive and accountable democratic structure, in contrast to other experiences. Individualization can be reduced through the union's emphasis on communality, collective action and solidarity.

Connecting with Other Struggles

It is through the union that probation officers can make links with other workers and with wider struggles within the state. Organization in the working-class form of the trade union facilitates these links. It also helps probation officers escape from an esoteric identity as 'the neutral professional' to a recognition of their status as sellers of labour power, having common cause with members of the working-class. These links enable us to connect with, and contribute to, broad and fundamental struggles over social justice, distribution of wealth, eradication of poverty and provision of welfare services. It may also provide opportunities to take our concerns about criminal justice issues into the working-class movement.

NAPO is as yet at a fairly rudimentary stage of development as a trade union. It was able to join with other public sector unions in opposition to the cuts in public services initiated by the 1974–9 Labour government. Similar opposition to the present Tory cuts has been hampered by NAPO's failure so far to secure independent affiliation to the TUC. Some branches have affiliated to local trades councils and have participated in local campaigns.

IN CONCLUSION

We have now put forward our suggestions for progressive work in personal practice, in the agency and in the union. We have limited ourselves to prescriptions which directly relate to our analysis, in search of the consistency which has been lacking in formulations of radical practice. We hope our ideas will stimulate discussion and regard them as a contribution to an unfinished debate. We have set out the limitations and potential in the role of probation officer but practitioners will still have to weigh these factors and decide on what they regard as appropriate action. So we conclude with a set of questions which we hope will help in that process.

- How can I respond progressively to this situation/ problem/task? What can I do here? Does this highlight important areas for struggle? What are they?
- Can my role be used in a progressive way here? Do possibilities arise from my position? What are the limitations of my role?

- How can this struggle be carried on in personal practice? In the agency? In the union? In connection with other groups? Which should be given priority?
- Does this require short-term or long-term action? Or both? Is now the appropriate time to engage in this struggle?
- How important is this issue? How much energy should I give it? What should my level of involvement be – a major role or lending support?
- Does this give me the opportunity to air important arguments or engage in significant debates or struggles?
- What alliances are possible? What are the limits of such alliances? What constraints will they impose?
- How does this fit in with other demands? How can I most effectively use my time? Does it involve risks to my position? What takes priority?
- What are the limitations and contradictions, what is the potential of the approach I have selected?

Notes

CHAPTER 1: SOMETHING'S WRONG

1. Brian Munday, 'What is Happening to Social Work Students?', *Social Work Today*, Vol. 3, No. 3, 1972.
2. Ibid.
3. Peter Bibby, 'Can Colleges Educate and Train Social Workers?', *Probation Journal*, Vol. 23, No. 1, 1976.
4. Ibid.
5. F.V. Jarvis, Chief Probation Officer's Address to Staff Meeting, 4 Nov. 1977 (unpublished).
6. Ibid.
7. David Mathieson, 'Conflict and Change in Probation', *Probation Journal*, Vol. 22, No. 2, 1975.
8. L.V. Coates, 'Reflections on a Differential Treatment Plan', *Probation Journal*, Vol. 21, No. 3, 1978.
9. David Millard, 'The Obligation to Risk', *Probation Journal*, Vol. 25, No. 3, 1978.
10. P. Priestley, J. McGuire, D. Flegg, V. Helmsley and D. Welham, *Social Skills and Problem Solving*, Tavistock Publications, 1978.
11. NAPO Members Action Group, *Probe* (Single Salary Scale Special Issue), Sept. 1977.
12. Ibid.
13. *Report of the Working Party on Management Structure in the Probation and After-Care Service*, Para. 114, 1980 (unpublished).

CHAPTER 2: COURT-BASED WORK

1. Home Office, *National Activity Recording Study*, 1977.
2. J. Thorpe, *Social Enquiry Reports: A Survey*, Home Office Research Study No. 48, 1979.
3. *Report of the Inter-Departmental Committee on the Business of the*

Criminal Courts (Streatfeild Report), Cmnd 1289, HMSO, 1961.

4. D. Mathieson and A. Walker, *Social Enquiry Reports*, Probation Paper No. 7, National Association of Probation Officers, 1971.

5. Pat Carlen and Margaret Powell, 'Professionals in the Magistrates' Courts; the Courtroom Lore of Probation Officers and Social Workers', in *Social Work and the Courts*, ed. Howard Parker, Edward Arnold, 1979.

6. F.V. Jarvis, *Probation Officer's Manual*, Butterworth, 1974.

7. Joan King, *The Probation and After-Care Service*, Butterworth, 1969.

8. F.V. Jarvis, L.V. Coates and F.P. Hutchinson, 'Development of a Court Intake and Assessment Team', *Probation Journal*, Vol. 25, No. 2, 1978.

9. D. Mathieson and A. Walker, *Social Enquiry Reports*.

10. Ibid.

11. Martin Davies and Andrea Knopf, *Social Enquiry Reports and the Probation Service*, Home Office Research Study No. 18, 1973.

12. F.G. Perry, *Information for the Court: A New Look at Social Enquiry Reports*. University of Cambridge Institute of Criminology, 1974.

13. Ibid.

14. J. Thorpe, *Social Enquiry Reports: A Survey*.

15. Alec Samuels, 'The Probation Service and its Relationship with the Magistracy', *Justice of the Peace*, No. 140, 1976.

16. Ian Pearce and Anne Wareham, 'The Questionable Relevance of Research into Social Enquiry Reports', *Howard Journal*, Vol. 16, No. 2, 1977.

17. F.G. Perry, *Reports for Criminal Courts*, Owen Wells, 1979.

18. Ian Pearce and Anne Wareham, 'The Questionable Relevance of Research into Social Enquiry Reports'.

19. F.G. Perry, *Information for the Court*.

20. F.G. Perry, *Reports for Criminal Courts*.

21. S. Brody, *Research into the Aims and Effectiveness of Sentencing*, Home Office Research Study No. 35, 1975.

22. Ian Pearce and Anne Wareham, 'The Questionable Relevance of Research into Social Enquiry Reports'.

23. Ibid.

24. Pauline Hardiker, 'The Role of the Probation Officer in Sentencing', in *Social Work and the Courts*, ed. Howard Parker, Edward Arnold, 1979.

25. Pat Carlen and Margaret Powell, 'Professionals in the Magistrates' Courts'.

26. Ibid.

27. Home Office, *National Activity Recording Study*.

28. *Report of the Departmental Committee on the Probation Service* (Morison Report), Cmnd 1650, HMSO, 1962.

29. Ibid.

30. Ibid.

31. *Probation of Offenders: The Probation Rules*, Statutory Instrument 723, HMSO, 1965.

32. Ibid.

33. *Report of the Departmental Committee on the Probation Service*, 1962.

34. CCETSW, *Learning to be a Probation Officer*, Report of a Study Group on Practice Placements in the Probation and After-Care Service, Paper 18, 1978.

35. F.V. Jarvis, *Probation Officer's Manual*.

36. Mark Monger, *Casework in Probation*, Butterworth, 1972.

37. Joan King, *The Probation and After-Care Service*.

38. *Report of the Departmental Committee on the Probation Service*, 1962.

39. Mark Monger, *Casework in Probation*.

40. R. Foren and R. Bailey, *Authority in Social Casework*, Pergamon, 1968.

41. Central Council of Probation and After-Care Committees, 'The Diminished Use of the Probation Order', *National Association of Probation Officers Newsletter*, Nov. 1978.

42. Home Office, *National Activity Recording Study*.

43. Nottingham Probation and After-Care Service, 'Community Service Consumer Survey 1973–76' (unpublished).

44. Philip Bean, *Rehabilitation and Deviance*, Routledge & Kegan Paul, 1976.

45. Central Council of Probation and After-Care Committees, 'The Diminished Use of the Probation Order'.

46. Reported in the *Guardian*, 15.9.79.

47. National Association of Probation Officers, *Young Adult Offenders: A Statement of Policy in Response to the Report of the Advisory Council on the Penal System*, 1975, (unpublished).

48. Geoffrey Pearson, 'Making Social Workers', in *Radical Social Work*, eds Roy Bailey and Mike Brake, Edward Arnold, 1975.

49. Paul Corrigan, *Schooling the Smash Street Kids*, Macmillan, 1979.

50. R. Foren and R. Bailey, *Authority in Social Casework*.
51. Geoffrey Parkinson, 'I give them money', *New Society*, 5.2.70.
52. Nottingham Probation and After-Care Service, 'Community Service Consumer Survey'.
53. Geoffrey Parkinson, 'I give them money'.
54. Bill Beaumont, 'A Supportive Role', *Probation Journal*, Vol. 23, No. 3, 1976.
55. Henry Giller and Alison Morris, 'Supervision Orders: The Routinisation of Treatment', *Howard Journal*, Vol. 17, No. 3, 1978.
56. Nottingham Probation and After-Care Service, 'Community Service Consumer Survey'.
57. Mark Monger, *Casework in Probation*.
58. Geoffrey Parkinson, 'I give them money'.
59. Geoffrey Pearson, 'Making Social Workers'.

CHAPTER 3: PRISON-BASED WORK

1. Joint Negotiating Committee for the Probation and After-Care Service, *Report of the Working Party on Pay Structure*, 1979, (unpublished).
2. *Report of the Committee on Discharged Prisoners' Aid Societies* (Maxwell Report), Cmnd 8879, HMSO, 1953.
3. *Report of the Advisory Council on the Treatment of Offenders. The Organisation of After-Care*, HMSO, 1963.
4. Home Office Circular 130/67.
5. F.V. Jarvis, *Probation Officer's Manual*, Butterworth, 1974.
6. *Prison Rules*, Statutory Instrument 388, HMSO, 1964, 1971.
7. Home Office Discussion Paper, *Social Work in the Custodial Part of the Penal System*, 1974.
8. *Committee of Enquiry into the United Kingdom Prison Services*, (May Report), Cmnd 7673, HMSO, 1979.
9. *Probation Officers in Prisons*, A Report of the Treatment of Offenders Committee of the National Association of Probation Officers, NAPO, 1971.
10. *The Work of Probation Officers in the Welfare Departments of Prisons*, A Report by a Working Party of the National Association of Probation Officers, NAPO, 1976.
11. Ibid.
12. Ibid.
13. Brian Stokes, 'Probation Officers in Penal Institutions', in

Pressures and Changes in the Probation Service, ed. Joan King, Cropwood Conference Series No. II, 1979.

14. *The Work of Probation Officers in the Welfare Departments of Prisons.*
15. Ibid.
16. Ibid.
17. Mike Othen, 'Prison Welfare – Time to Think Again?', *Probation Journal,* Vol. 22, No. 4, 1975.
18. *Probation Officers in Prisons.*
19. Mike Othen, 'Prison Welfare – Time to Think Again?'.
20. M. Shaw, *Social Work in Prison,* Home Office Research Study No. 22, HMSO, 1974.
21. A.J. Fowles, *Prison Welfare: An Account of an Experiment at Liverpool,* Home Office Research Study No. 45, HMSO, 1978.
22. Mike Othen, 'Prison Welfare – Time to Think Again?'.
23. David Smith, 'Probation Officers in Prisons', in *Creative Social Work,* eds D. Brandon and B. Jordan, Blackwell, 1979.
24. John Tracey, 'Ongoing Casework in a Local Prison', *Probation Journal,* Vol. 18, No. 1, 1972.
25. Mike Othen, 'Prison Welfare – Time to Think Again?'
26. R.A. Hutchinson, 'Politically Motivated Prisoners – The Welfare Approach', *Probation Journal,* Vol. 24, No. 3, 1977.
27. Philip Bean, *Rehabilitation and Deviance,* Routledge & Kegan Paul, 1976.
28. *Probation Officers in Prisons.*
29. 'Crime and Punishment: John McVicar Looks Back', *The Listener,* 8.3.79.
30. *Probation Officers in Prisons.*
31. Mike Othen, 'Prison Welfare – Time to Think Again?'
32. *The Work of Probation Officers in the Welfare Departments of Prisons.*
33. Phyllida Parsloe, 'After-Custody: Supervision in the Community in England, Wales and Scotland', in *Social Work and the Courts,* ed. Howard Parker, Edward Arnold, 1979.
34. *Probation Officers in Prisons.*
35. R.A. Hutchinson, 'Politically Motivated Prisoners – The Welfare Approach'.
36. Martin Davies, *Prisoners of Society,* Routledge & Kegan Paul, 1975.
37. *The Work of Probation Officers in the Welfare Departments of Prisons.*
38. *Report of the Advisory Council on the Treatment of Offenders.*

39. Phyllida Parsloe, 'After-Custody: Supervision in the Community in England, Wales and Scotland'.
40. *Report of the Advisory Council on the Treatment of Offenders*.
41. F.V. Jarvis, *Probation Officer's Manual*.
42. *Report of the Advisory Council on the Treatment of Offenders*.
43. Ibid.
44. Ibid.
45. *Prison and Borstal After-Care: Annual Report of the Council of the Central After-Care Association*, HMSO, 1962.
46. *Report of the Advisory Council on the Treatment of Offenders*.
47. Phyllida Parsloe, 'After-Custody: Supervision in the Community in England, Wales and Scotland'.
48. *The Adult Offender*, White Paper, Cmnd 2852, HMSO, 1965.
49. Joan King, *The Probation and After-Care Service*, Butterworth, 1969.
50. F.V. Jarvis, *Probation Officer's Manual*.
51. *Young Adult Offenders. A Report of the Advisory Council on the Penal System* (Younger Report), HMSO, 1974.
52. *Youth Custody and Supervision – A New Sentence*, Cmnd 7406, HMSO, 1978.
53. *Young Offenders*, White Paper, Cmnd 8045, HMSO, 1980.
54. Home Office, *National Activity Recording Study*, 1977.
55. I. Sinclair, M. Silberman, B. Chapman and A. Leissner, *Explorations in After-Care*, Home Office Research Study No. 9, HMSO, 1971.
56. Martin Davies, *Prisoners of Society*.
57. *Young Adult Offenders: An Examination of the Younger Report by a Working Party of the London Branch of NAPO*, 1975.
58. Martin Davies, *Prisoners of Society*.
59. Ibid.
60. Phyllida Parsloe, 'After-Custody: Supervision in the Community in England, Wales and Scotland'.
61. Martin Davies, *Prisoners of Society*.
62. Phyllida Parsloe, 'After-Custody: Supervision in the Community in England, Wales and Scotland'.
63. Martin Davies, *Prisoners of Society*.
64. Phyllida Parsloe, 'After-Custody: Supervision in the Community in England, Wales and Scotland'.
65. A.E. Bottoms and F.H. McClintock, *Criminals Coming of Age*, Heinemann, 1973.
66. *Young Adult Offenders: An Examination of the Younger Report by a Working Party of the London Branch of NAPO*.

67. Ibid.
68. Martin Davies, *Prisoners of Society*.
69. Robin Parker and Brian Williams, 'Probation Officers and Parole Supervision', *Probation Journal*, Vol. 23, No. 4, 1976.
70. Phyllida Parsloe, 'After-Custody: Supervision in the Community in England, Wales and Scotland'.
71. Ibid.
72. Home Office, *National Activity Recording Study*.
73. Martin Davies, *Prisoners of Society*.

CHAPTER 4: NEW DEVELOPMENTS

1. Robert Carr, in the foreword to *The Criminal Justice Act 1972: A Guide for the Courts*, Home Office, 1972.
2. *Non-Custodial and Semi-Custodial Penalties: Report of the Advisory Council on the Penal System* (Wootton Report), HMSO, 1970.
3. *The Criminal Justice Act 1972: A Guide for the Courts*.
4. National Association of Probation Officers, *Community Service Orders – Practice and Philosophy*, 1980.
5. *The Criminal Justice Act 1972: A Guide for the Courts*.
6. Elizabeth Burney, *A Chance to Change. Day Care and Training for Offenders*, Howard League, 1980.
7. Criminal Justice Act 1972, Para. 53.
8. Home Office, *The Probation and After-Care Service in a Changing Society*, Central Office of Information, 1977.
9. *The Criminal Justice Act 1972: A Guide for the Courts*.
10. Elizabeth Burney, *A Chance to Change*.
11. Letter from the Home Secretary to NACRO, 22.12.79.
12. Northumbria Probation and After-Care Service, *Wayside Project Review 1976/77*.
13. Elizabeth Burney, *A Chance to Change*; West Yorkshire Probation and After-Care Service, *Day Activity Group Review 1976/7 and 1977/8*; Probation and After-Care Service, Midland Region, Staff Development Office, *Workshop for those Establishing Day Centres*, 1980.
14. Sally Burningham, 'Members of an Exclusive Club', *Health and Social Service Journal*, 9.6.78; John Roberts, Brief Information about the Barbican Centre, Jan. 1979, (unpublished).
15. M. Shaw, S. Brody and K. Heal, 'Crime Policy Planning. Some Selected Research Findings', *Home Office Research Bulletin* No. 6, 1978.

16. Letter from the Home Secretary to NACRO, 22.12.79.
17. Roy Bailey, 'Employment Finding – a Key Resource in Probation Work', *Apex News*, Oct. 1978.
18. *Report of the Chief Officer, Nottinghamshire Probation and After-Care Service, Beaver Project, 1979.*
19. J.N. Birkbeck, 'Barnsley Community Workshop. A New Approach to the Unemployed Offender', *Probation Journal*, Vol. 27, No. 3, 1980.
20. Inner London Probation and After-Care Service, *Bulldog Manpower Services Ltd (Supported Work Project). Report on third year 1977/8.*
21. Keith Taylor, 'YOP for Young Offenders', *Youth in Society*, April 1979; Margaret Clode, 'Opportunities for Those "At Risk" ', *Actions*, May 1979.
22. David D. Smith, 'Impact – The Major Findings', *Home Office Research Bulletin No. 4*, 1977; M.S. Folkard, D.E. Smith and D.D. Smith, IMPACT *Volume II*, Home Office Research Study No. 36, 1976.
23. 'Alternative Methods of Working in a Probation Setting', West Midlands Probation and After-Care Service Day Conference Programme (unpublished).
24. 'Report of the Elizabeth Fry Day Centre', St Mary's House, Nottingham (unpublished).
25. Roger Shaw, 'The Persistent Sexual Offender – Control and Rehabilitation ', *Probation Journal*, Vol. 25, No. 1, 1978.
26. Douglas Bell, 'Scunthorpe Cycling Group', *Probation Journal*, Vol. 26, No. 3, 1979.
27. P. Priestley, J. McGuire, D. Flegg, V. Helmsley and D. Welham, *Social Skills and Problem Solving*, Tavistock Publications, 1978.
28. Ibid.
29. 'The Leicestershire Probation Service Package', *Apex News*, October 1978 (adapted from a report by Malcolm Jones, project co-ordinator).
30. L.V. Coates, 'Reflections on a Differential Treatment Plan' *Probation Journal*, Vol. 21, No. 1, 1974.
31. Angela Glendenning, 'Probation: The Team, the Office, the Community', *National Association of Probation Officers Newsletter*, August 1977.
32. Central Bristol Area Team Probation Project, Starve the Borstals Workshop, 5/6 April 1979, (unpublished); Preston West Team, 'Putting the Sacred Cows Out to Grass', *Probation*

Journal, Vol. 24, No. 3, 1977.

33. F.V. Jarvis, L.V. Coates and F.P. Hutchinson, 'Development of a Court Intake and Assessment Team', *Probation Journal*, Vol. 25, No. 2, 1978.

34. Elizabeth Wilson, *Women and the Welfare State*, Tavistock Publications, 1977.

35. D.S. Palmer, 'The World of the Probation Hostel', University of Cambridge Institute of Criminology, Cropwood Study, 1978 (unpublished).

36. Central Bristol Area Team Probation Project.

37. Elizabeth Burney, *A Chance to Change*.

38. 'The Leicestershire Probation Service Package', *Apex News*.

39. Sue Winfield, 'What Has the Probation Service Done to Community Service?,', *Probation Journal*, Vol. 24, No. 4, 1977.

40. Kent Probation and After-Care Service, 'Medway Day Training Centre', *Treatment Within the Community*, 1980.

41. Bruce Hugman, *Act Natural*, Bedford Square Press, 1977.

42. M. Hurley, 'The Sheffield Detached Unit – Report to Magistrates' 11.9.78 (unpublished).

43. *The Criminal Justice Act 1972: A Guide for the Courts*.

44. D.S. Palmer, 'The World of the Probation Hostel'.

45. Colin Lawson, *The Probation Officer as Prosecutor*, University of Cambridge Institute of Criminology, Cropwood Study, 1978.

46. Central Bristol Area Team Project.

47. National Association of Probation Officers, *Community Service Orders – Practice and Philosophy*.

48. W.H. Pearce, 'Day Training Centre: Proposals for the Establishment of a Day Centre within the Area of the Inner London Probation and After-Care Committee', 1973 (unpublished).

49. Jane Andrews, 'Adult Probation Hostels', *Home Office Research Bulletin* No. 4, 1977; K. Pease, S. Billingham and I. Earnshaw, *Community Service Assessed in 1976*, Home Office Research Study No. 39, 1977.

50. Kent Probation and After-Care Service, 'Medway Day Training Centre'.

51. Stan Cohen, 'Community Control – A New Utopia', *New Society*, 15.3.79.

CHAPTER 5: THE RADICAL CRITIQUE

1. Geoffrey Pearson, *The Deviant Imagination*, Macmillan, 1975.
2. Ibid.
3. *Case Con* Manifesto, reproduced as an appendix in *Radical Social Work*, eds R. Bailey and M. Brake, Edward Arnold, 1975.
4. John Connor, 'Casework – Antidote to Bolshevism', in *The Best of Case Con*, 1977.
5. Crescey Cannan, 'The Ideology of Casework and Professionalism', in *The Best of Case Con*, 1977; Geoffrey Pearson, 'The Politics of Uncertainty', in *Towards a New Social Work*, ed. H. Jones, Routledge & Kegan Paul, 1975.
6. Elizabeth Wilson, 'Sexist Ideology of Casework', in *The Best of Case Con*, 1977.
7. Irwin Epstein, 'The Politics of Behaviour Therapy: the New Cool-out Casework?', *Towards a New Social Work*, ed. H. Jones, Routledge & Kegan Paul, 1975.
8. For example: Bill Rolston, 'Iron Fists . . . Kid Gloves', in *The Best of Case Con*, 1977; Marjorie Mayo, 'Community Development: A Radical Alternative?', *Radical Social Work*, eds R. Bailey and M. Brake, Edward Arnold, 1975; Crescey Cannan, 'Welfare Rights and Wrongs', in *Radical Social Work*, eds R. Bailey and M. Brake, Edward Arnold, 1975.
9. *Case Con* Manifesto.
10. Mike Simpkin, *Trapped within Welfare*, Macmillan, 1979.
11. Richard Herne, 'LA Community Workers', in *The Best of Case Con*, 1977.
12. *Case Con* Manifesto.
13. Bob Deacon, 'Perspectives for *Case Con*', in *The Best of Case Con*, 1977.
14. *Young Adult Offenders. A Report of the Advisory Council on the Penal System* (Younger Report), HMSO, 1974.
15. Tony Holden, 'The Younger Report – What Price Probation?', *Probe*, July 1974.
16. *Young Adult Offenders. An Examination of the Younger Report by a Working Party of the London Branch of NAPO*, 1975.
17. Ibid.
18. Ibid.
19. NAPO Members' Action Group, Working Document, agreed NMAG Conference February 1976 (unpublished).
20. Ibid.

21. Thomas Mathieson, *The Politics of Abolition*, Martin Robertson, 1974.
22. *Home Office Working Party on Vagrancy and Street Offences*, Working Paper, HMSO, 1974.
23. Philip Bean, *Rehabilitation and Deviance*, Routledge & Kegan Paul, 1976.
24. Campaign for Academic Freedom and Democracy, *The Attack on Higher Education. Where Does it Come From? A Reply to the Gould Report* (undated).
25. J. Gould *et al.*, *The Attack on Higher Education: Marxism and Radical Penetration*, Institute for the Study of Conflict, 1977.
26. Ron Lewis, 'Artful Dodgers of the World Unite', in *The Black Papers on Education*, eds C.B. Cox and R. Boyson, Methuen, 1977.
27. Donald Bell, 'NAPO and NMAG', *National Association of Probation Officers Newsletter*, April 1977.
28. F.V. Jarvis, Chief Probation Officer's Address to Staff Meeting, 4.11.77 (unpublished).
29. Robert Pinker, 'Slimline Social Work', *New Society*, 13.12.79.
30. Brian Munday, 'What is Happening to Social Work Students?', *Social Work Today*, Vol. 3, No. 3, 15.6.72.
31. Stan Cohen, 'It's All Right for You to Talk: Political and Sociological Manifestos for Social Action', *Radical Social Work*, eds R. Bailey and M. Brake, Edward Arnold, 1975.
32. Gary Clapton, 'Radicalism – What Does It All Add Up To?', *Social Work Today*, Vol. 8, No. 28, 19.4.77.
33. Geoffrey Mungham, 'Social Workers and Political Action', in *Towards a New Social Work*, ed. H. Jones, Routledge & Kegan Paul, 1975.
34. John Armstrong and Kevin Gill, 'What Relevance for Community Work?', *Social Work Today*, Vol. 10, No. 11, 7.11.78.
35. BASW, *The Social Work Task. A BASW Working Party Report*, 1977.
36. Edwin Schur, *Radical Non-intervention*, Prentice-Hall, 1973.
37. A.E. Bottoms and W. McWilliams, 'A Non-Treatment Paradigm for Probation Practice', *British Journal of Social Work*, Vol. 9, No. 2, 1979.
38. Paul Halmos, *The Personal and the Political: Social Work and Political Action*, Hutchinson, 1978.
39. Ibid.
40. Ibid.
41. Bill Jordan, 'Know Your Wrongs', in *The Best of Case Con*, 1977.

42. Bill Jordan, *Freedom and the Welfare State*, Routledge & Kegan Paul, 1976.
43. Bill Jordan, *Helping in Social Work*, Routledge & Kegan Paul, 1979.
44. Bill Jordan, *Freedom and the Welfare State*.
45. Bill Jordan, *Helping in Social Work*.
46. Bruce Hugman, 'Radical Practice in Probation', in *Radical Social Work and Practice*, eds M. Brake and R. Bailey, Edward Arnold, 1980.
47. Ibid.
48. Ibid.
49. Cynthia Cockburn, *The Local State: Management of Cities and People*, Pluto Press, 1977.
50. Elizabeth Wilson, *Women and the Welfare State*, Tavistock Publications, 1977.
51. Ian Gough, *The Political Economy of the Welfare State*, Macmillan, 1979.
52. Norman Ginsburg, *Class, Capital and Social Policy*, Macmillan, 1979.
53. Chris Jones, 'Social Work Education 1900–77', in *Social Work, Welfare and the State*, eds N. Parry, M. Rustin and C. Satyamurti, Edward Arnold, 1979.
54. P. Corrigan and P. Leonard, *Social Work Practice under Capitalism: A Marxist Approach*, Macmillan, 1978.
55. Stuart Hall, Chas Critcher, Tony Jefferson, John Clarke and Brian Roberts, *Policing the Crisis: Mugging, the State and Law and Order*, Macmillan, 1978.
56. National Deviancy Conference and Conference of Socialist Economists, *Capitalism and the Rule of Law: From Deviancy Theory to Marxism*, Hutchinson, 1979; National Deviancy Conference, *Permissiveness and Control. The Fate of the Sixties Legislation*, Macmillan, 1980.
57. John Clarke, 'Critical Sociology and Radical Social Work: Problems of Theory and Practice', in *Social Work, Welfare and the State*, eds N. Parry, M. Rustin and C. Satyamurti, Edward Arnold, 1979.
58. Norman Ginsburg, 'Crisis in Social Work Education. What Crisis?', *Bulletin of Social Policy*, No. 4, autumn 1979.
59. John Clarke, 'Critical Sociology and Radical Social Work'.

CHAPTER 6: TOWARDS A MARXIST CRITIQUE

1. The starting points for new theorists have been the works of A. Gramsci, L. Althusser, N. Poulantzas and R. Miliband.

2. For more detail, see Ian Gough, *The Political Economy of the Welfare State*, Macmillian, 1979 (especially chapter 2); Norman Ginsburg, *Class, Capital and Social Policy*, Macmillan, 1979 (especially chapter 2).

3. *The Wealthy*, CIS Report No. 25.

4. For more detail, see Paul Corrigan and Peter Leonard, *Social Work Practice under Capitalism*, Macmillan, 1978 (especially chapter 8); Ian Gough, *The Political Economy of the Welfare State* (especially chapter 4).

5. Karl Marx and Frederick Engels, *Manifesto of the Communist Party*, Pathfinder Press, 1970.

6. Ralph Miliband, *Marxism and Politics*, Oxford University Press, 1977.

7. *The Wealthy*, CIS Report No. 25.

8. Ibid.

9. For more detail, see Ian Gough, *The Political Economy of the Welfare State* (especially chapter 3).

10. For more detail, see S. Hall, C. Critcher, T. Jefferson, J. Clarke and B. Roberts, *Policing the Crisis: Mugging, the State and Law and Order*, Macmillan, 1978; Norman Ginsburg, *Class, Capital and Social Policy*; Cynthia Cockburn, *The Local State*, Pluto Press, 1977.

11. Further reading: London Edinburgh Weekend Return Group, *In and against the State: Discussion Notes for Socialists*, CSE Books, 1979; CSE State Group, *Struggle over the State*, CSE Books, 1979.

12. CSE State Group, *Struggle over the State*, CSE Books, 1979. See also S. Hall *et al.*, *Policing the Crisis*.

13. For more detail, see S. Hall *et al.*, *Policing the Crisis*; Cynthia Cockburn, *The Local State*; Elizabeth Wilson, *Women and the Welfare State*, Tavistock Publications, 1977; Paul Corrigan and Peter Leonard, *Social Work Practice under Capitalism*.

14. S. Hall *et al.*, *Policing the Crisis*.

15. Ibid.

16. S. Hall, *Drifting into a Law and Order Society*, The Cobden Trust, 1980.

17. For more detail, see A. Gramsci, *Selections from the Prison Notebooks*, eds and translators Q. Hoare and G. Nowell

Smith, Lawrence & Wishart, 1971; S. Hall *et al.*, *Policing the Crisis;* S. Hall, *Drifting into a Law and Order Society.*

18. Paul Corrigan, 'The Welfare State as an Arena of Class Struggle', *Marxism Today,* March 1977.

19. C. Jones and T. Novak, 'The State and Social Policy', in *Capitalism, State Formation and Marxist Theory,* ed. Phillip Corrigan, Quartet Books, 1980.

20. Ibid.

21. Gareth Stedman-Jones, *Outcast London,* Oxford University Press, 1971.

22. C. Jones and T. Novak, 'The State and Social Policy'. For further reading, see Paul Corrigan, 'The Welfare State as an Arena of Class Struggle'; C. Jones and T. Novak, 'The State and Social Policy'; Gareth Stedman-Jones, *Outcast London;* Peter Keating (ed.), *Into Unknown England 1866–1913,* Fontana, 1976.

23. Paul Corrigan, 'The Welfare State as an Arena for Class Struggle'; Ramesh Mishra, 'Marx and Welfare', *The Sociological Review,* Vol. 23, No. 2, 1975.

24. Norman Ginsburg, *Class, Capital and Social Policy.*

25. C. Jones and T. Novak, 'The State and Social Policy'.

26. Ibid.

27. CSE State Group, *Struggle over the State* (chapter 6).

28. Paul Willis, *Learning to Labour: How Working-Class Kids get Working-Class Jobs,* Saxon House, 1977.

29. For further reading on the way welfare services capital, see C. Jones and T. Novak, 'The State and Social Policy'; Cynthia Cockburn, *The Local State* (chapter 2); Elizabeth Wilson, *Women and the Welfare State;* Norman Ginsburg, *Class, Capital and Social Policy;* Ian Gough, *The Political Economy of the Welfare State.*

30. Elizabeth Wilson, *Women and the Welfare State.*

31. For more details, see Elizabeth Wilson, *Women and the Welfare State;* Cynthia Cockburn, *The Local State;* Paul Corrigan and Peter Leonard, *Social Work Practice under Capitalism.*

32. Karl Marx, *Capital,* Vol. 1, chapter 7, Penguin, 1976.

33. Douglas Hay, 'Property, Authority and the Criminal Law', in *Albion's Fatal Tree,* D. Hay, P. Linebaugh, J. Rule, E.P. Thompson and C. Winslow, Peregrine, 1977.

34. For further reading, see Karl Marx, *Capital;* Douglas Hay, 'Property, Authority and the Criminal Law'; S. Hall *et al., Policing the Crisis;* M. Ignatieff, *A Just Measure of Pain,*

Macmillan, 1978.

35. S. Hall *et al.*, *Policing the Crisis*.
36. Ibid.
37. Sol Picciotto, 'The Theory of the State, Class Struggle and the Rule of Law', in *Capitalism and the Rule of Law*, National Deviancy Conference and Conference of Socialist Economists, Hutchinson, 1979.
38. Douglas Hay, 'Property, Authority and the Criminal Law'.
39. Reported in *The News Line*, 14.6.80.
40. For more reading, see S. Hall *et al.*, *Policing the Crisis*; Sol Picciotto, 'The Theory of the State, Class Struggle and the Rule of Law'; Frank Pearce, *Crimes of the Powerful: Marxism, Crime and Deviance*, Pluto Press, 1976.
41. For a more detailed argument, see Carol Smart, *Women, Crime and Criminology: a Feminist Critique*, Routledge & Kegan Paul, 1976.
42. Jock Young, 'Mass Media, Drugs and Deviance', in *Deviance and Social Control*, eds P. Rock and M. McIntosh, Tavistock Publications, 1974.
43. S. Hall *et al.*, *Policing the Crisis*.
44. Ralph Miliband, 'Class War Conservatism', *New Society*, 19.6.80. For more reading, see Campaign against a Criminal Trespass Law, *Whose Law and Order?*, Jan. 1979; S. Hall *et al.*, *Policing the Crisis*.
45. S. Hall, *Drifting into a Law and Order Society*.
46. For more detailed reading, see Jock Young, 'Left Idealism, Reformism and Beyond: From New Criminology to Marxism', in *Capitalism and the Rule of Law*, National Deviancy Conference of Socialist Economists, Hutchinson, 1979; S. Hall *et al.*, *Policing the Crisis*; S. Hall, *Drifting into a Law and Order Society*; Frank Pearce, *Crimes of the Powerful*.
47. S. Hall *et al.*, *Policing the Crisis*.
48. For further reading, see Sol Picciotto, 'The Theory of the State, Class Struggle and the Rule of Law'; Boaventura de Sousa Santos, 'Popular Justice, Dual Power and Socialist Strategy', in *Capitalism and the Rule of Law*, National Deviancy Conference and Conference of Socialist Economists, Hutchinson, 1979.
49. S. Hall *et al.*, *Policing the Crisis*.
50. Douglas Hay, 'Property, Authority and the Criminal Law'.
51. Ibid.; Mike Fitzgerald, *Prisoners in Revolt*, Penguin, 1977; Peter Linebaugh, 'the Tyburn Revolt Against the Surgeons',

in *Albion's Fatal Tree*, D. Hay *et al.*, Peregrine, 1977.

52. S. Hall *et al.*, *Policing the Crisis*.
53. Jock Young, 'Left Idealism, Reformism and Beyond'.
54. For detail, see S. Hall *et al.*, *Policing the Crisis*; Michael Ignatieff, *A Just Measure of Pain*.
55. Mike Fitzgerald, *Prisoners in Revolt*.
56. For further reading, see Michel Foucault, *Discipline and Punish: The Birth of the Prison*, Peregrine, 1979; Mike Fitzgerald, *Prisoners in Revolt*; Michael Ignatieff, *A Just Measure of Pain*.

CHAPTER 7: PROBATION: A MARXIST CRITIQUE

1. Michel Foucault, *Discipline and Punish: The Birth of the Prison*, Peregrine, 1977.
2. Ibid.
3. John Clarke, 'Social Democratic Delinquents and Fabian Families', in *Permissiveness and Control. The Fate of the Sixties Legislation*, National Deviancy Conference, Macmillan, 1980.
4. Michel Foucault, *Discipline and Punish*.
5. *Probation of Offenders: The Probation Rules*, HMSO, 1965.
6. Colin Lawson, *The Probation Officer as Prosecutor*, University of Cambridge Institute of Criminology, Cropwood Study, 1978.
7. Elizabeth Burney, *A Chance to Change: Day Care and Training for Offenders*, Howard League, 1980.
8. D.S. Palmer, 'The World of the Probation Hostel', University of Cambridge Institute of Criminology, Cropwood Study 1978 (unpublished).
9. Geoffrey Pearson, *The Deviant Imagination*, Macmillan, 1975.
10. Paul Corrigan, *Schooling the Smash Street Kids*, Macmillan, 1979.
11. For example: 'Alternative Methods of Working in a Probation Setting', West Midlands Probation and After-Care Service Day Conference Programme (unpublished); 'Report of the Elizabeth Fry Day Centre', St Mary's House, Nottingham (unpublished).
12. Michel Foucault, *Discipline and Punish*.
13. *Report of the Departmental Committee on the Probation Service* (Morison Report), Cmnd 1650, HMSO, 1962.
14. For example: Greater Manchester Probation and After-Care

Service: 'Priority Areas of Work', March 1980 (unpublished); 'Probation and Alternatives to Custody', Discussion Document from the Professional Committee of NAPO, March 1980; Colin Lawson, *The Probation Officer as Prosecutor;* A.E. Bottoms and W. McWilliams, 'A Non-Treatment Paradigm for Probation Practice', *British Journal of Social Work,* Vol. 9, No. 2, 1979; M. Bryant, J. Coker, B. Estlea, S. Himmel and T. Knapp, 'Sentenced to Social Work?', *Probation Journal,* Vol. 25, No. 4, 1978; Robert J. Harris, 'The Probation Officer as Social Worker', *British Journal of Social Work,* Vol. 7, No. 4, 1977; Kent Probation and After-Care Service, *Treatment Within the Community,* 1980; Elizabeth Burney, *A Chance to Change; Young Adult Offenders: Report of the Advisory Council on the Penal System* (Younger Report), HMSO, 1974; *Youth Custody and Supervision: A New Sentence,* Cmnd 7406, HMSO, 1978.

15. London Edinburgh Weekend Return Group, *In and Against the State: Discussion Notes for Socialists,* CSE Books, 1979.

16. Home Office, *The Probation and After-Care Service in a Changing Society,* Central Office of Information, 1977.

17. Geoffrey Parkinson, 'I give them money', *New Society,* 5.2.70.

18. Paul Corrigan, *Schooling the Smash Street Kids.*

CHAPTER 8: TOWARDS UNDERSTANDING

1. London Edinburgh Weekend Return Group, *In and Against the State: Discussion Notes for Socialists,* CSE Books, 1979.

2. Kent Probation and After-Care Service, 'Close Support Unit', *Treatment Within the Community,* 1980.

3. Kent Probation and After-Care Service, Probation Control Unit (job outline for Probation Control Unit Officer), 1980 (unpublished).

4. Ibid.

5. CSE State Group, *Struggle Over the State,* CSE Books, 1979; *Where is Lucas Going?,* CIS Report No. 12. Lucas Aerospace Shop Stewards Combine Committee, *Lucas, An Alternative Plan,* IWC Pamphlet No. 55.

6. Thomas Mathieson, *The Politics of Abolition,* Martin Robertson, 1974.

CHAPTER 9: SOCIALIST PROBATION PRACTICE

1.   A.E. Bottoms and W. McWilliams, 'A Non-Treatment Para-
     digm for Probation Practice', *British Journal of Social Work*, Vol.
     9, No. 2, 1979.
2.   See for instance: Ros Coward, 'Rereading Freud: The Making
     of the Feminine', *Spare Rib*, May 1978; Fiona McKay, 'Self-
     Help Therapy', *Spare Rib*, July 1976; Frances Seton, 'Opening
     Myself to Change', *Spare Rib*, March 1976. For an example
     from outside the Women's Movement see: *Red Therapy*, pro-
     duced by Red Therapy, c/o 28 Redbourne Avenue, London
     N3, 1978.
3.   A.E. Bottoms and W. McWilliams, 'A Non-Treatment Para-
     digm'.
4.   'A Non-Treatment Paradigm for Probation Practice', Con-
     ference at Tapton Hall, Sheffield, 28–30 March 1980 (un-
     published papers).
5.   'Juveniles Subject to Police Surveillance', *The Leveller*,
     January 1980; 'Police Called in to Search out School Truants',
     Guardian 30.9.80; John Alderson, *Policing Freedom*, Macdonald
     & Evans, 1979; Labour Campaign for Criminal Justice,
     Community Policing, 1980; Ann Blaber, *The Exeter Community
     Policing Consultative Group*, NACRO, 1979.
6.   Victoria Greenwood and Jock Young, *Abortion in Demand*,
     Pluto Press, 1976.
7.   Mick Ryan, *The Acceptable Pressure Group*, Saxon House, 1978.
8.   *Young Adult Offenders: A Report of the Advisory Council on the
     Penal System* (Younger Report), HMSO, 1974.

Index

215